MW01277897

America's Answer

Addressing The Terrorist Threat At Its Generative Source

J. Patrick Griffin, Jr.

PRESS

America's Answer
by J. Patrick Griffin, Jr.

Printed in the United States of America

Library of Congress Control Number: 2002110765
ISBN 1-594671-94-X

Unless otherwise indicated, Bible quotations are taken from
the New King James Version. Copyright © 1982 by Thomas
Nelson Publishers.

Xulon Press
www.XulonPress.com

Xulon Press books are available in bookstores everywhere,
and on the Web at www.XulonPress.com.

"J. PATRICK GRIFFIN, JR., is a self-taught student of world affairs, and a previously published author. His writings, which address a variety of contemporary issues in religion and geopolitics, are acclaimed by his readers for their originality and depth."

"H.L. SOKOL, is the inventor of Infinity Picture, a unique photo-enhancement device. He served with the 115th Infantry Regiment from Omaha Beach to the river Elbe, Germany. This regiment was featured in the movie, *Saving Private Ryan*. Sokol earned a purple heart at St. Lo, France; a bronze star and a silver star at Julich, Germany.

Table of Contents

Part One: Can Our Current Measure of Response Accomplish
Our Objectives?
1. Pounding the Body Without Reaching the Soul
The bombing campaign in Afghanistan is bruising our enemies, yet without defeating them psychologically. A survey
of the popular response in several nations. The resolve of the
terrorists, rather than wilting under our show of power, is
intensifying. The militant movement is a violent struggle for
the control of who will define Islam, and who will determine
the relationship of Islam to government and society. Until we
raise the magnitude of our strategy, we will not effectively
address this problem at its generative source.
2. Creating Fear in the Suicide Fighter
. A psychological profile of the suicide fighter. By the proper
strategy, fear can be created in the minds of the people who
had persuaded themselves of a personal immunity to fear.
The moment confronts us with a need to debate the form
and magnitude of a truly effective response.
Part Two: What Confronts Us
3. Historical Survey of the Islamic Militant Movement
An overview of its history. The three-fold goal: An
Islamist purification of the Middle East, the collapse of

Foreword

On July 5, 1943, I answered my country's call to defend the world against a foe who dreamed of bending every knee under the lordship of his doctrine. As the soldiers splashed through the cold, bloody seawater along Omaha and Utah beaches on June 6, 1944, we had an ocean at our back and a monster in our face. The hellish noise of artillery, bullets and airplanes numbed our fear as each man fed his heart on the stench of gunpowder and the hatred of Nazism. Every inch of our advance was purchased with blood, but the full force of our situation registered with me only when a dear buddy went down in "no-man's-land." We were in the midst of a severe firefight; no one seemed to respond to his painful cries for help. I left my senses and sprinted to a contorting form bleeding badly from a shrapnel wound in the stomach. A set of bulging eyeballs burned an image into my pupils and left me a different man. I cradled his head on my lap, attempting to stem the flow of blood from his wounds. Gurgling through red spit, he choked out, "Herb, please don't let me die!" I assured him the medic was coming and I would stay with him. Within moments, accompanied by sounds I have never forgotten, the young soldier lost his struggle! But thanks to such heroes America did not lose hers.

Several weeks later, during intense fighting near St. Lo,

I went down with a wound that would take me out of battle but would not threaten my life. While I recuperated in England it seemed unjust that I would return to enjoy the beauty of a free and bountiful country while my buddy was slowly turning to dust in his grave. I came back from Europe with a new appreciation for life, and with a deep sense of honor for having spent my blood in the service of America as she struggled for the survival of civilization. We destroyed that enemy because there was *no other way* of eliminating the total threat he posed to our people and to our way of life. We sometimes did things unpleasant to remember, but none of us has an apology to offer. America accomplished what the times required of her, and *because* we stepped up to be counted as a force in human history we preserved and expanded the sphere of personal freedom across half the earth.

On the morning of September 11, 2001, a hideous creature, more vile than Hitler himself (who could have imagined!), awoke us from a twelve-year stupor in which the laurels of having won the Cold War were more important to our leadership than the rising scepter of a new kingdom of evil. I fumed with the frustration of an aged stallion whose instincts were calling him to a race in which he could no longer compete. Thousands of Americans and scores of foreign guests had been slaughtered in a religious crusade inspired by hate-driven imams and funded by oil-filthy sheiks. I discerned from the outset that this struggle for our children's tomorrow would not be won through a form of warfare that any of us had previously imagined. When our president later promised a "patient accumulation of successes" I feared that our leadership was not studying the problem at its core level.

This new enemy has a source of inspiration beyond the reach of our bullets, and he entertains no doubts as he seeks to fulfill the mandate of his Prophet and the tradition of his people. This enemy descends upon us at the vanguard of the most viciously crusading movement in human history, having commenced with waves of murderous zealots pouring out of Arabia in the seventh century and swearing by the tip of their swords that every knee on earth would bow to the doctrine of a man with a nine-year old wife. Within decades they had cast their killing shadow across all tribes and nations as far as the borders of India in the east and Greece in the north, and westward to the Atlantic shores of Morocco. Having conquered, occupied and consolidated the reign of their religion, at a faster pace than any army had ever advanced, the invaders set their sights on Christian civilization and took Spain in a heartbeat. The next morning, as it were, they were pouring across the Pyrenees and sailing into the waterways of France with shouts of victory in the name of their god. In AD 732, the valiant army of Charles Martel halted the Muslim advance and Europe was temporarily saved from the crusading soldiers of the most successful imperialistic movement in history; having been turned back for the first time, they went to their newly conquered homes and studied patience.

In an opportune time they crossed into southeastern Europe and captured the great city of Constantinople, converting the stronghold of Caesars and Patriarchs into a Mosque-State with a charter for world domination. By the early seventeenth century they had killed their way through the Balkans, and in the process introduced to the world a new word: "Slave!" The forced servitude of peoples under the Islamic domination reached a new crescendo as the thick-boned and blond-headed Slavs of the Balkans presented a new appeal to the Muslim lords. Multitudes of Slavic women and very young girls were imprisoned in harems while their husbands, brothers, sons and fathers served the remainder of their lives in chains. So many Slavs were thus exploited by the crusading Muslims that "slavery" became the commonly used word for a condition of forced servitude!

By the early seventeenth century the Islamic expansion had penetrated to the gates of Europe's soul as the horde of crusaders descended on the crucial city of Vienna. Here, for the second time (but not for the final), the civilization associated with Christianity came perilously close to annihilation under the sword of Islam. The invaders were turned back on the strength of the newly emerging capacities of an embryonic "modern" Europe. Once again they were forced to retreat and to devise some new plot for fulfilling their Prophet's mandate of total subjugation of the earth under the dominion of their religion.

For several centuries after their stunning defeat at Vienna the Muslim world decayed and collapsed under the flawed logic of rejectionism. By rejecting the empowering forms of knowledge evolving among the northern peoples, who were slowly liberating their minds and their lives from ancient concepts of authoritarian control, the civilization of Islam handed itself a fundamental disadvantage from which it showed no promise of ever recovering. But it has not abandoned its core political concept of "constant war" *until*, as their holy writings command, the pagans are all beheaded and the Christians live in silent servitude, and "the Jews will hide behind trees and stones, and the trees and the stones will speak and say, 'Muslim, behind me is a Jew; come and kill him!'" As a Hamas leader boasted some years ago (quoted in the 12/18/92 issue of the Wall Street Journal): "The war is open until... the last Jew in the world is eliminated." And as the Palestinian sheik, Abu Halabaya, preached not so long ago in a live broadcast from a Gaza City Mosque: "In any country wherever you are, kill the Jews and the Americans!" And from the putrid mouth of Bin Laden: "We call on every Muslim who believes in Allah and wishes to be rewarded to comply with Allah's order to kill the Americans and plunder their money whenever and wherever [they may be found]."

And from the Ayatollah Khomeini after the Islamic Revolution in Iran: "The governments of the world should know that... Islam will be victorious in all the countries of the world!"

The centuries-long pause in Islam's reach for world domination was widely misinterpreted as a peaceful change in its nature. We, the West, who are so quickly to let down our guard and to naively impute our good intentions to the character of those who aim to destroy us, fell asleep on the top of our mountain as the Trojan Horses moved into our neighborhoods and the creeping spiders wove webs of horror throughout the realm of slumber! Now that the web is cast and the horses have emptied their bellies into places-of-waiting across America and throughout the civilized world, we are waking up fast to the reality that the parenthetical era of peaceful coexistence with Islam was not due to a changing of its nature at all. Rather, it was the maturing of its wisdom as it patiently obeyed its founder's commandment to "make peace with your enemy until you are strong enough to annihilate him!" Centuries of peaceful coexistence has lulled us into forgetting the warning issued by Mohammad and recorded in Surah 5, verse 51 of the Koran: "O you who believe! Do not take the Jews and the Christians for friends... whoever amongst you takes them for a friend, then surely he is one of them!" Thankfully, a majority of Muslims in America and Europe do not consistently obey the doctrine of Mohammad. Without acknowledging it themselves, they have fashioned an alternative version of Islam which allows them to live peacefully and productively in the free and modern world. Muslims of this class are a thriving part of what America promises to all who will subscribe to its founding principles. Unfortunately, and on a chilling scale, mingling among the multitudes of alternative Muslims are the murderous groups who strive to obey Mohammad consistently, and who are thereby compelled to pledge constant war against all who do not subscribe to *their* founding principles.

What is America's *Answer* to such a threat? How do we articulate a framework of concepts that will guide us toward the development of a truly decisive *answer*? I am soberly pleased to announce to America that Patrick Griffin has untied the Gordian Knot by a resistance-crushing display of original insights and battlefield logic that would make the famous WWII Commanding General, George S. Patton, proud! As I read my way through a copy of his stunning work, *America's Answer*, in one sitting, I felt under my feet the bloody-wet sands of Normandy and I saw before my eyes the hideous face of an enemy who *will* go down in permanent defeat!

Patrick Griffin, who was once my student but has now surpassed me in his excellence, has seized the conceptual beachhead of America's war on terror by showing that he not only understands the core nature of this current conflict, but also that he understands the nature of its only realistic solution. His arguments, at times, are profoundly disturbing, as he strips away the facades to show us what will be required if the terrorist threat is to be eliminated rather than merely restrained. As he stated in a recent radio interview aired out of Fresno, California:

"After more than a year of mobilizing enormous national resources in the fight against terror, all we have managed is to hold our enemy at the line of scrimmage!"

Mr. Griffin argues that this is not progress, and that the War on Terror cannot be won until America raises the magnitude of its strategy and attacks the enemy where it lays open and vulnerable to total defeat!

The subtitle of his book, quite appropriately, is *Addressing The Terrorist Threat At Its Generative Source*, and I place myself in firm agreement with the assessment of author and retired Army Lieutenant Colonel Ralph Peters, who says in his cover endorsement of *America's Answer:* "Vigorous, principled and provocative, this is one book that is not afraid to take a stand! Mr. Griffin challenges every reader to re-examine his or her beliefs about the contemporary world."

A recent article in TIME Magazine, by Michael Elliot, was titled: *Why The War On Terror Will Never End.* The article goes far in making the case for what many Americans already fear and believe: The U.S. Government has made a lot of photo-ops in this struggle, but the War on Terror is not *really* being won!

Mr. Elliot's article also observes that for most Americans, "winning the war on terrorism means a clear victory over al Qaeda." I am not alone in testifying that *America's Answer* presents an aggressively reasoned formula for precisely such a victory. Although many other books on Islamic terrorism have been written since 9/11, to my knowledge there are none that advance a comprehensively thought-out strategy for attacking the problem at its root, and for annihilating it. On this score, *America's Answer* stands in a class all by itself! It is my expectation that this book will have a profound and highly controversial impact on the national discussion over issues pertaining to Islamic terrorism, and I commend Patrick Griffin for such a bold and timely contribution to our country in this time of extreme distress for civilization. Don't just read *America's Answer*, review it again, discuss it with your friends, get copies for others, take it to your school or college, discuss it with your teacher or professor and ask if *America's Answer* can be a special class assignment. Send a copy to your representative in your state or Washington DC! Use *America's Answer* as a reference when calling radio or TV talk shows.

As I conclude the writing of the Forward, I have great difficulty seeing the keyboard on my laptop; tears well up in my eyes and words are barred from my throat as the voice of my beloved comrade's blood cries out to me from the cold sands of Normandy, as again I must hear his awful guttural sounds of death, **"Herb, please don't let *America die!"***

This old soldier urges you; no, begs you: take the time, which is about what it takes to watch a movie or a sporting event, and read **America's Answer;** *it is really a* **"Handbook For Survival!"**

Lord, have mercy!

H. L. Sokol
June 6, 2003

Preface

An article in the November 28 issue of the *Wall Street Journal* poses the question bluntly: "If the U.S. nabs Osama bin Laden, dead or alive, will that cripple his organization's ability to mount further terrorist attacks?" The article goes on to cede that we cannot safely assume this:

> Eliminating Mr. bin Laden would cut off al Qaeda's head. . . . But new leaders could sprout, U.S. officials say, even if the successors lack the inspirational power of Mr. bin Laden. The U.S. could be forced to mount operations against terrorist commanders who aren't even known to investigators yet, and in countries far from Afghanistan.
>
> "This is not a situation where if you cut off the head you kill the beast," says Matthew Levitt, an analyst for the Federal Bureau of Investigation. . . . "If all the al Qaeda leaders were found hiding in one cave in Afghanistan, you'd still have cells remaining in Yemen, Spain, the U.S., and many others."

After the crumbling of the Taliban frontlines during

the third and fourth weeks of November, commentator George F. Will reported in the November 26 issue of *Newsweek:* "Now there is a danger of . . . thinking that the war on terrorism is now a mere mopping-up operation. . . . In Germany last week, in an unusual public meeting of senior officials from German and U.S. investigative and intelligence agencies . . . [it was made known] that at least 70,000 Islamic fundamentalists have passed through Al-Qaeda's terrorist-training camps in the last few years."

Alain Grignard, a Belgian expert on Islamic terrorism, was quoted in the November 19 issue of the *Los Angeles Times:* "They have succeeded in creating a very motivated core that is present everywhere."

Al Qaeda members relish the fact of the covert global presence they have established over the past decade. The October 29 issue of the *Washington Post National Weekly Edition* provided excerpts from a bugged conversation between two members of an al Qaeda cell operating in Milan. In that conversation, a thirty-three-year-old Tunisian named Khemais boasted: "Al Qaeda exists from Algeria to the Philippines. They're everywhere." The *Post* article went on to report: "Most of those in the Frankfurt and Milan cells, including Khemais . . . are now in custody, but the Italian documents make clear that the European terrorist ranks are easily replenished with recruits."

Homeland Security Director Thomas Ridge also has warned that other terrorists are "waiting in the wings" to replace Osama bin Laden. And Gerald F. Seib wrote for the *Wall Street Journal* on November 14: "Even in this hour of success, though, it's worth bearing in mind a more troubling long-term problem. In brief, it is this: The broader Islamic world will remain a veritable incubator of more Osamas if today's trends aren't reversed. . . . There are hundreds of millions of young Muslims out there: even if Osama bin Laden goes away, they won't."

In an interview during the third week of November, as Taliban positions were collapsing and the Northern Alliance was rapidly gaining control of the country, bin Laden acknowledged his days were likely numbered—but not his movement: "The Americans think they will solve this problem by killing me [actually, we do not think that] . . . But it's not easy to solve this problem. This war has been spread all over the world" (from the *Post Weekly,* November 19).

We can continue accumulating battlefield victories, finishing in one country and moving on to another, and then another, and then another. There is no question as to the superiority of our armed forces, or of our ability to place other significant obstacles in the way of the terrorist program. Their plentiful funding, ease of movement, front-street training camps, and the unsuspecting posture of their target have all changed drastically since September 11. Future terrorist activity will be much more difficult to carry out. We have slowed the program down, and yet our anxiety remains because we know we have not stopped it.

We are achieving our government's stated goal of a "patient accumulation of successes." But are these material successes getting at the *generative core* of the enemy? Former U.S. Senator Sam Nunn has explained how the psychological factor is the root issue which our material successes are not necessarily addressing: "Until this psychological war is waged effectively, we will eliminate 10 terrorist cells but do it in a way that creates 20 new ones; that is not progress. . . . This psychological war is the key to whether our children and grandchildren will be plagued years from now" (quoted by Albert R. Hunt in the October 25 issue of the *Wall Street Journal*).

This book is an offering of knowledge and ideas to America. It is, on one hand, a display of my own psychological interaction with events as they have developed since

September 11. I began this work on the night of October 26, during the height of the anthrax crisis. The book was completed on December 17. Over the span of these eight weeks, major changes have emerged within the Central Asian Theater. The reader will observe how some of the issues are now old and several entirely outdated. Yet the book can also be viewed as a running diary, illustrating the development in my own thinking as I attempted to process the succession of events and arrange them into a coherent view of how the world was changing. The following pages are therefore an articulated expression of my efforts to understand the situation from a perspective that developed within a timeframe ending in late December. Obviously, as with any thinking person, my perspective on many of the issues will receive adjustments and fine tunings with the passage of time and with the development of unforeseeable events. Yet I am confident my main thesis will endure the test of tomorrow.

Since September 11, my mental engagement of the issues has been proactive as well as reactive. I have wanted to understand not only the nature of the conflict, but also what the most effective course of action might be for achieving a comprehensive solution. To think intelligently in this direction obviously requires a substantial context of related knowledge, and an analysis of numerous critical sub-themes. With this in mind, the following pages provide a set of historical sketches, such as:

1. A narrative of the development of militant Islam since the early 1950s in Egypt,

2. A sweeping history of Israel since 63 BC,

3. A survey of Russian political history since the tenth century, and

4. Pointed observations on the U.S. conquest of
America in the nineteenth century and of the
Arab takeover of the Middle East during the
seventh century.

The historical briefings add to the supporting context
for the main thesis. Although the current scope and magnitude of our war effort is deeply bruising the body of our
enemy, I do not believe it is reaching to the generative level.
My book advances a formula aimed at solving the terrorist
problem precisely at this level.

Our leadership has asked for a contribution of some
sort from every American, as in Attorney General John
Ashcroft's call for "each American to help us defend our
nation in this war." This writing is my own attempt to
answer Mr. Ashcroft's call commensurately with my very
limited abilities and opportunities. Who can say where the
next useful idea might come from? If my labor comes to
nothing, I will at least have done my best to bring a meaningful contribution to my country in a time of distress.

The book consists of eighteen progressive articles
converging on the main thesis. There are numerous important sub-developments, such as my thoughts on the role of
Israel and on the future of democracy. But each development
is written with a view to the central concept.

If at times the complexion of the writing is harsh, it
is a consequence of holding my logic strictly to the most
immediate issues at hand. Enormous suffering is going on in
the world. We will never wash away all the tears, or comfort
all the fears, but if we can at least move things in that direction, we will have shown ourselves to be a great generation.
Yet before we can address the suffering, we must first
destroy the enemy who stands in the way of all other posi-
tive possibilities. To accomplish this, we must locate the
fatal vulnerability of those assaulting us, and we must

aggressively hold them hostage at this point.

In summary, this book is an attempt to articulate a framework of knowledge and ideas for public debate on how best to pursue a swift liquidation of the *generative energies* driving a global organization of mass murderers. I believe my formula is viable, realistic, and necessary.

Author

Excerpt from Newspaper Article, January 30, 1942

In an interview on "Good Morning Nippon," a Japanese bomber pilot wounded over Pearl Harbor denounces the American Navy's attempt to defend itself from the attack.

"They should have accepted our bombs as divine will," says Murama Takaji, 22, who appears on the popular morning show with both arms in a sling. He says that once he recovers he hopes to join the elite Divine Wind [kamikaze] squadron. "It would be a great honor to crash into an American ship," he says. "I hear there are many pretty geishas in the next life."

—Quoted by Christopher Buckley, *Wall Street Journal*, November 5, 2001.

Introduction

Our success in the past century with the militant civilization of Japan informs us that doubt and fear can be
created in people who had persuaded themselves of a personal immunity to such experiences.

Until we reduced Hirohito from a god to a man,
Japanese civilization had been the most fanatically militant
on earth, shocking the world with its brutality and its
resolve, not least in the form of suicide fighters ending their
lives in spectacular airplane crashes against Allied positions.
Since that war was decisively concluded fifty-six years ago,
Japan has refused to send a single soldier into combat.
Along with our material successes on those fearsome battlefields of World War II, we destroyed the generative core of
an enemy that had pledged itself *and the name of its god* to
our destruction.

The cruelty and the imperialistic ambitions of the
religio-militant Japanese state were on a par with what
the Nazis had exhibited until the death of their own leader
earlier that summer, yet there was one important difference. The Germans believed their leader was a great man,
whereas the Japanese believed theirs was a god. Our
success in producing a fundamental change in the religiously conditioned attitude of the war-era Japanese did

not transform them into an irreligious society, but it did compel them to become civilized, modern, and peaceful. After blindly obeying a militant religious leader, they were compelled to understand the value of thinking for themselves, and also to recognize the insanity of believing their god would give them world domination.

The Japanese have become our enduring friends, as have the Germans. But sensitivity to our friends should not hinder us from aggressively analyzing their comprehensive defeat in our search for lessons that might assist us in the confrontation with today's enemy. World War II was a different time and a different war, yet there are important analogies that we do well to exploit in our effort to understand the vulnerabilities of the enemy who threatens us now.

Islamic radicals have linked their concept of God to their campaign of death against Americans. We can certainly beat them on the battlefields, one after another, across the face of the earth. We can impose economic obstacles to the funding of their program, sting operations to round up suspects and wannabes, and diplomatic pressures to complicate their global support system. But we cannot prevent this entity's replication of its internal components until we attack it at the generative level.

Al Qaeda, and the far-reaching terrorist movement it represents, is staggering under the international assault led by America. We are pounding hard on the body, yet without penetrating to the marrow.

In dealing with an enemy of any sort, the imperative is to discover that enemy's vulnerability, and to attack him at this level. The vulnerability of the Islamic terrorist movement has nothing to do with a fear of personal death, but is rather related to its concept of God. Until we address our enemy at this level, the sub-world of Islamic militancy will continue replicating leaders, recruits, and plans (with more difficulty, of course, but not without successes that will draw blood from deep within our collective body).

How do we succeed against an enemy with a necrophilic obsession about death, especially his own? The terrorists believe, and have shown a horrific willingness to act on this belief, that their own death in the name of Allah is merely a passageway into the sexual pleasures of the Paradise of which they have been told. In linking the erotic impulse to their fascination with death, they have trans-formed murder itself into a terrifying religion. Although they run from our guns and bombs, it is not because they are afraid to die. They simply hate us, and cannot tolerate the thought of dying without simultaneously inflicting death upon us. Abu-Ghaith, a principal spokesman for al Qaeda, boasted: "The Americans must know that the storm of air-planes will not stop, and there are thousands of young peo-ple who look forward to death like the Americans look forward to living." Osama bin Laden exulted: "To America, I say only a few words to it and its people: I swear to God that America will not live in peace." And Mullah Omar pre-dicted: "We will see this [the destruction of America] in a short time. . . . The plan is going ahead, and God willing, it is being implemented. . . . If God's help is with us, this will happen within a short period of time. Keep in mind this prediction."

The only certified means of destroying this sense of invulnerability, and thereby creating doubt in a mind that had once been convinced by its own myth of immunity, is an encounter with something on a scale which that mind had previously been unwilling to imagine. I do not believe the form of warfare we have prosecuted in Afghanistan, how-ever impressive on its own scale, and however ferocious from the perspective of many in the world, is able to produce such an encounter with the type of enemy confronting us.

We must search into deeper places for the soft spot of this enemy. This place of vulnerability will not be reached by pounding the mountains of Tora Bora, the deserts of Iraq, the jungles of the Far East, or any of the other terrorist resorts throughout the world (and what of Paris, London, Hamburg, Milan, etc.?). When we are willing to boldly identify the mental vulnerability of this particular enemy, and to attack him decisively at this spot, the war will be over.

My objective in this book is to urge thinking and discussion in the direction of more aggressive and promising solutions to the threat confronting us. Our "patient accumulation of successes" offers no realistic hope of ever destroying the *inner source* of this terrorist threat. Until this plague is eliminated at its generative core, we will continue suffering from its revolting and lethal presence on the earth.

In the middle of the last century, America and its allies were confronted with an enemy that required unprecedented American audacity to defeat. The leaders of that generation boldly formulated a logic of destruction that promised to crush the psychology of the enemy, and they implemented their logic with no apologies. They were not hamstrung by concerns for political correctness or the fear of an unclean finale.

Today we are confronted with an enemy even more fanatical than the Nazis or the war-era Japanese. We cannot ultimately defeat this enemy without doing things that make us uncomfortable. There is no such thing as a clean response to an act of war, and this is more emphatically true in the context of our present situation. We do well to recall that even the Great War conducted by "The Greatest Generation" was far from clean. In our talking seriously of a decades-long war against the terrorists, we are effectively promising our children and grandchildren the inheritance of a plague we could have eliminated at any time in the last ten years. In doing this, we are suggesting a legacy of generational puerility in the far shadows of that Greatest Generation, which had no intention of handing *their* children an unfinished job.

Today's enemy relies on the strategies of asymmetrical warfare, with potential access to devices of destruction that could hurt us in ways we do not like to think about. This enemy is able to recruit suicide fighters *at will*, and has every intention of perpetuating and escalating its campaign of terror. My book is an attempt to develop a framework of knowledge and ideas for public debate on what would be involved in a U.S.-led response that would dissolve the Islamic terrorist movement at the psychological level.

Part One:

Can Our Current Measure of Response Accomplish Our Objectives?

1.   Pounding the Body Without Reaching the Soul

The terrorists are not seriously intimidated by what is currently being done in Afghanistan. Although it is a difficult experience for them, their fear of these bombs is perhaps the near equivalent of a softer person's fear of firecrackers.

As I write, we are nearly a month into our intense bombing campaign in Afghanistan. Any person following the daily news is aware of how the general Islamic response, from Egypt to Indonesia, and from Pakistan to Saudi Arabia, is one of intensifying hatred against America. The terrorists are not only unbowed by the deluge of bombs, but their spiritual resolve to destroy us is stronger than ever, and their support among the Muslim population throughout the Middle East and beyond increases daily. The same principle has been well illustrated in the situation with Iraq. Egyptian President Hosni Mubarak once told the *Los Angeles Times:* "The more you bomb Sadaam Hussein, the stronger he gets."

Our ongoing bombing of Iraq certainly weakens Sadaam militarily, but it also strengthens both his personal resolve and his support among the Iraqi people and the Arab world in general. Nothing in the past month suggests that, in this respect, the bombing of Afghanistan is proving more effective than the bombing of Iraq. Although the Taliban will eventually crumble under our assault, the strengthening international support for them is undeniable.

In Indonesia, the situation is increasingly unstable because of the growing support for bin Laden among the Muslims in that Far Eastern nation. Before the bombing began, Indonesian President Megawati had assured President Bush of her country's support in the war against terrorism. It is now unlikely that Megawati will be able to deliver on her promise in any substantial manner. The radical Muslim leadership in Indonesia is fanning the flames, and the al Qaeda operatives in that country are deploying their sophisticated organizational skills toward the goal of overthrowing the democratically elected government and replacing it with a fundamentalist Islamic regime. It is extremely improbable that the fundamentalists will succeed in overthrowing the Indonesian democracy. But their hand is so strengthened by the rhetoric surrounding the U.S. bombing of the Taliban that the resources of the Megawati government will be critically distracted by the civil strife in her nation of more than two hundred million people. The escalation of anti-American sentiment in Indonesia has become so threatening that many regions in that country are unsafe for U.S. citizens.

In Pakistan, thousands of Pakistani Taliban supporters are grabbing their rifles and crossing the border to fight and—many of them hope—to die with their Muslim brothers in "holy war" against the U.S. military. On October 28, the *Los Angeles Times* reported: "An estimated 8,000 armed Pakistani volunteers massed at their country's rugged northwestern border, ready to join the Taliban inside Afghanistan . . . armed with rocket launchers and Kalashnikov rifles. . . [The Pakistanis marching into Afghanistan were urged on by graffiti slogans on village walls, saying] 'It is your duty to kill. . . Arms are the jewelry of pious Muslims.' [The militants themselves declared:] 'If the government tries to stop us, we will declare a jihad against Pakistan. . .We are obligated to kill everyone who obeys Jews and Christians and disregards Muslims, even if they are from our own country.'"

Pakistan is ruled by a military dictatorship that controls a small nuclear arsenal and the production capacity to build more. When a concerned Western journalist recently asked Pakistani "President" Musharraf if his country's nuclear weapons would be safe in the event of a massive fundamentalist uprising, Musharraf sought to assure the journalist that Taliban supporters would never get their hands on Pakistan's nuclear weapons. Of course, Musharraf had to say this, yet it is known that many Taliban supporters are within the Pakistani military, including some among the highest ranks. This is very disturbing, and grows increasingly so with time.

In Iran, the U.S. actions in Afghanistan have strengthened the anti-American conservatives in their contest with the moderate president, Mohammed Khatami. The *Los Angeles Times* reported: "Iranian Defense Minister Ali Shamkhani said Iran was 'ignoring anti-American sentiments' rising in the Muslim world in the wake of the attacks on Afghanistan and called for a return to the radical ideals of the late revolutionary leader Ayatollah Khomeini. . . President Mohammed Khatami's position appears to be weakening, with growing unrest in Iran and with human casualties mounting in Afghanistan."

Shakani's reference to "the anti-American sentiments rising in the Muslim world in the wake of the attacks on Afghanistan" is particularly revealing, since Iran has been a long-time enemy of the Taliban. Our war effort in Afghanistan is uniting the sympathies of our enemies, and is serving to powerfully fuel the fundamentalists' vision of a pan-Islamic state that would then hope to impose the choice of Sharia or death on all who fall within its sphere.

In Saudi Arabia, the government is deeply concerned about the growing support for bin Laden in its own country. The *Los Angeles Times* reported in its September 26 issue: "Saudi Arabia remains reluctant to provide military support to a U.S.-led antiterrorism campaign, a move it fears would anger legions of Saudis who support the regime in Kabul [the Taliban]. . . Saudi officials . . . are well aware that militant Islamist feeling runs high in the kingdom, and that any use of Saudi territory to wage war against fellow Muslims could provoke outright unrest. Stability in tightly controlled Saudi Arabia is crucial for the global economy: Any serious upheaval in the world's biggest oil producer would disturb international energy markets, crippling industries world-wide and quickly spreading turmoil across the region."

In a remarkably informative Special Report featured in the October 15 issue of *Newsweek,* writer Fareed Zakaria explained: "The biggest Devil's bargain has been made by the moderate monarchies of the Persian Gulf, particularly Saudi Arabia. The Saudi regime has played a dangerous game. It deflects attention from its shoddy record at home [referring to the royal family's notorious lack of Muslim piety] by funding religious schools (madrasas) and centers that spread a rigid, puritanical brand of Islam—Wahhabism [the version of Islam adhered to by Osama bin Laden]. In the past 30 years Saudi-funded schools have churned out tens of thousands of half-educated, fanatical Muslims who view the modern world and non-Muslims with great suspicion. America in this world view is almost always evil."

Michael Vlahos, a former director of the Center for the Study of Foreign Affairs at the U.S. State Department, explained in the November 8 issue of *Rolling Stone* magazine: "The enemy hopes to draw strength from the American retaliation. If Muslim regimes that acquiesce and support America can be painted as betrayers of Islam, then the insurgent's authority can only grow."

The initial phase in the planned terrorist agenda involves an overthrow of the Middle Eastern governments that do not cooperate with the fundamentalist view of Islam and its role in society and the world. These governments are perceived by the terrorists as puppet regimes that could not retain their power without Western military and intelligence support (as a general rule, this is an accurate perception). In this respect, the terrorist movement is first of all an insurgency, a violent struggle for the control of who will define

Islam, and who will determine the relationship of Islam to government and society.

This gives an important insight into the calculation of the terrorists in their attack on September 11. They were certain the United States would retaliate militarily (although they grossly underestimated the magnitude and determination of our response), and they gambled that America's retaliation would serve to mobilize and focus the anger of tens of millions of disaffected Muslims throughout the Middle East and beyond. By every indication, they have gambled with at least some measure of success. Yet in all of this they were, and are, dismissing as irrelevant the fact that we have a capacity to destroy what they value most—and what they are, in fact, fighting for. Although they are unafraid of death, there would be little appeal in dying if they were assured it would jeopardize the existence of the symbol of all they are fighting for. By taking the threat of our capacity to this level, we will have reached their place of vulnerability, and we will have undermined the rationale for the campaign of martyrdom.

The Taliban is widely despised throughout Afghanistan, yet an increasing contempt for the U.S. has also developed since the bombing began on October 7. This was illustrated in stunning fashion when Abdul Haq, an important Afghani resistance leader, slipped into Afghanistan on October 21 and attempted to rally support in his own tribal area. Haq was an adored hero and leader among his people, but the bombings have generated such a profound animosity that he was unsafe even in his home base. The *Los Angeles Times* reported in its October 28 issue: "[It took] 2-1/2 days to reach Haq's home village of Azra. . . At each stop, Haq drew large gatherings, but the discussions were heated. According to one of Haq's comrades on the trip, people were bitter about the killings of civilians by U.S. bombings and skeptical about any plan that the U.S. supported."

After we destroy the Taliban and the bombings stop, what will become of the anti-U.S. rage among these Afghan people and of the anger of millions of Muslims throughout the world? Although the people of Afghanistan will be grateful for their liberation from the rule of the Taliban, we should not be so naïve as to imagine these liberated Afghani Muslims will then begin loving America.

Haq was one of the greatest of the mujahedin leaders in the war against the Soviets, a hero of immense status among the Afghan people. But the rising hatred against America eclipsed the love for Abdul Haq, and he was betrayed in his own tribal area. The Taliban was alerted to his whereabouts, and he was captured just a few miles east of his hometown, Azra. Haq was quickly tried and executed by a gunshot to the back of the head. The *Times* recorded one analyst's observation: "[Haq's death] is a setback because it shows the strength of [anti-U.S. sentiment inside Afghanistan] . . . he couldn't even be protected in his own tribal area" (October 27 issue).

Is the current nature of our military effort accomplishing our larger long-term objectives? We have clearly weakened the Taliban's military capabilities, and the Special Forces being sent in are the most formidable fighting teams in the world. There is no question that our soldiers on the ground will destroy the Taliban positions wherever they find them. Yet by every indication, our campaign in Afghanistan is incubating further threats against us, and will continue to do so even after we have completely destroyed the Taliban.

After we have won on the battlefields of Afghanistan, we will have struck no meaningful fear into the hearts of other terrorists. We will not have destroyed, dismantled, or even intimidated "al-Qaeda." We will have only intensified their rage against us. Our victory in Afghanistan is likely to mean little more than the need to pursue similar victories in a host of other countries, from North Africa to the Indonesian archipelago. Each excruciating victory will create more numerous and more furious enemies in other places, and what will become of us in the process?

2.   Creating Fear in the Suicide Fighter

Among Islamic nations, suicide fighters now command the widespread glamour and adoration that we give to rock stars and movie actors.

In the Introduction, I noted from historical precedent that "fear can be created in the minds of people who had persuaded themselves of a personal immunity to fear."

A suicide fighter believes that he (or she) has developed an inner immunity to the fear of personal destruction. As a cultural phenomenon, the image of invulnerability exuded by the suicide fighter is the ultimate intoxicant for a young mind suffering under a sense of oppression and weakness. He stands in the midst of a downtrodden and frustrated people, presenting himself as fearless, unconquerable, and omnipotent. He is the symbol of everything they crave to be, and the religious leadership sanctifies his image of power by articulating a theology of Martyrdom and Paradise. The suicide fighter leaves one world in a flash of triumph, and enters another as a hero with an eternal franchise. He has his cake even after he eats it. He is assured the best of everything and he cannot lose. It is as abu-Ghaith boasted: "The Americans must know that the storm of airplanes will not stop, and there are thousands of young people who look forward to death like the Americans look forward to living."

The bombs we are exploding in Afghanistan are creating terror for women and children, and for individual men who have not sufficiently cultivated a narrative of personal immunity. As for the terrorists and their hard-core supporters, they are not intimidated by what we are doing.

There are reasons for their hatred of us, and in due time our society might want to engage in a boldly reasoned debate as to what our own responsibilities are for the accumulated hatred of America that has now reached a level of mob insanity. But my concern in this writing is with a more restricted and immediate sphere of interest. The most urgent reality confronting us is the fact that the mob is there, and it has gone insane with its hatred and with its belief that it can succeed in making us bleed until we capitulate to its demands. There is no effective reasoning with such a pitch of madness. The moment confronts us with a need to debate the form and magnitude of a truly effective response. I have absolutely no doubt that our nation and its allies are in pos- session of that response.

Part Two:

What Confronts Us

3.   Historical Survey of the Islamic Militant Movement

The difficulty is not in *locating* the fatal vulnerability of this enemy. The vulnerability is easy to determine. The challenge is to develop our own understanding of the need to address the enemy at this weak and fatal point.

The de facto government in Afghanistan, the Taliban ("Student Movement"), is harboring the current symbolic leadership of the international Islamic terrorist movement. This civilization of terror (which is therefore more properly understood as an *anti*-civilization) answers in every meaningful way to the definition of a mass movement. In the present context there is no need for anything more than a schematic review of the causes and the historical development of this anti-civilization.

It had its formative modern beginnings in Egypt during the Nassar era, after the European colonizers had withdrawn their armies and left the Arab peoples to work out a new direction for themselves (with a conditioning proviso: the oil must flow). Every experiment in social and economic development failed (socialism, enlightened monarchism, nationalism, etc.), not only on account of intrinsic cultural issues but equally on account of continued meddling by the Soviets and the West. The overriding concern of these latter two civilizations was for a reliable supply of oil, as it was clear that industrial and technological superiority were the principal keys to whatever the eventual outcome of the Cold War would be. The most convenient short-term policy for the northern powers (the Soviets and the West) was to support the regimes willing to cooperate with their own imperative interest (a reliable supply of reasonably priced petroleum).

When a quasi-democratic movement took control of Iran in the early 1950s, the new Iranian government seized control of its own oilfields, which had previously been in the hands of behemoth American and British oil companies. This created an alarming uncertainty for the Western governments. In 1953, the U.S. and British governments engineered an overthrow of the democratically elected government in Iran and installed Reza Pahlavi (the Shah) as a dictator-monarch (rather than a titular head) over the country. Reza Pahlavi was a cruel man, but he kept the oil flowing and thereby maintained the Western support that kept him in power. All the while, among the millions of struggling Iranian people, a complex of discontent, rage, and humiliation was boiling under the surface. The word on the streets was that Islam was the answer. All of the conditions for the launch of a radical mass movement with an absolutist religious philosophy were in place, and in 1979 the world was shaken by the Islamic revolution in Iran.

The success of the Shiite fundamentalists ripped a hole in the image of Western power, giving birth to a belief in new possibilities among the Sunni Muslims of other Middle Eastern nations. If purified Islam had conquered the West in Iran, surely it could also conquer in Egypt, in Saudi Arabia, and anywhere else. As the psychology was fueling itself, tens of thousands of Islamic warriors traveled to Afghanistan to fight with their co-religionists against the Soviets. They believed they could humble the Soviet Union just as the Vietnamese had humbled America. The mercenary fighters poured in from among the Arabs, Indonesians, Malaysians, Filipinos, Pakistanis, Indians, and Bosnians. In Afghanistan, these mostly young and impressionable Muslims were imbibed with a flaming theology of Jihad from Egyptian and Saudi intellectuals.

After the Soviets withdrew in 1989, the fundamentalist leaders in Afghanistan (none of whom were actually Afghans, but rather the Arab co-religionists of the Afghans) decided they would not allow the energy and momentum of their movement to terminate on the victory in Afghanistan. Two important names emerge at this time: Osama bin Laden and Ayman Zawahiri. Zawahiri, an Egyptian, was the decisive intellectual force in the development of the theological/ideological vision of the organization founded by bin Laden. This is al Qaeda, an Arabic word meaning "The Base." The *Washington Post National Weekly Edition,* in its October 1 issue, explained in an article by a team of its foreign correspondents: "When al-Qaeda was founded in Afghanistan in the late 1980s, Ayman Zawahiri was at the creation. . . [He] would eventually help supply bin Laden's organization with its globalist ideology. . . Bin Laden brought financial resources . . . and Zawahiri expanded the theological and philosophical base of their mission. When the Afghan war ended, the men realized they had the makings of something sustainable. Following Zawahiri's ideas, they turned their eyes back toward Egypt, and across the globe to the United States." The *Post* article goes on to explain: "After more than a decade at bin Laden's side, [Zawahiri] formally merged Egyptian Islamic Jihad [an extreme terrorist organization closely allied with the terrorist groups that assassinated Anwar Sadat in 1981 and slaughtered 58 vacationing tourists at an Egyptian resort in 1997] with his al-Qaeda to form a combined World Islamic Front for Jihad Against Jews and Crusaders [that is, governments of the nations dominated by Christians]. . . The group that once had formed around Sadat's murder was no longer satisfied with opposing the "iniquitous princes" in charge of the Arab world."

Al Qaeda, and the international terrorist movement that it sponsors and symbolizes, has achieved a string of terrorist, military, and political successes that has inflamed its confidence and expanded its vision to a scale that we can properly define as insane.

The heart of the terrorist movement, having linked

its concept of God to its success in the campaign of terror, has now inflated to absurd proportions, believing itself to be indestructible. For the terrorist leadership, the bombs exploding in Afghanistan are viewed as tools for mobilizing support among millions of frustrated Muslims disenfranchised in their own countries, from Indonesia to Algeria and from Pakistan to Yemen. An Article of Confession in its broader vision is the complete destruction of American civilization, which it sees as the fountainhead of secularism, the puppeteer of corrupt and oppressive Middle Eastern regimes, and the true power behind the survival and military success of its existential archenemy, Israel. The final phase in the vision of this terrorist anti-civilization is the purification of the entire world by a choice of Sharia or death for every human being.

Nancy DeWolf Smith, a member of the *Wall Street Journal*'s editorial board, wrote in the September 19 issue of the *Journal:* "But Afghanistan had become attractive to yet another group, the international Islamists, many of them political outlaws in their own countries, who hoped to take advantage of the chaos there to make Afghanistan the first state headquarters for world-wide revolution."

By 1994, Sudan was temporarily serving as the center of the developing vision and plan for a worldwide conquest by fundamentalist Islam (which does not recognize or tolerate any other interpretation of Islam). Rory Nugent, a researcher with extensive knowledge of "the trail of fundamentalist Islam," in the October 25 issue of *Rolling Stone* magazine, described his 1994 encounter with Osama bin Laden and Hassan al-Turabi (at that time the most influential Islamic leader in Sudan):

> By all accounts, Turabi had engineered and nurtured the Islamization of Sudan. His biggest trick was replacing civil law with sharia. . .

Believe me, he says, we're only at the beginning of Islam's march. Soon, many nations will become one. And God's voice will thunder. Sudan, he adds, is merely the staging area for the worldwide expansion of fundamentalist Islam. . . The fuel for the coming Islamic revolution is being bunkered as we sit and talk, Turabi informs me. From earlier discussions, I know he's referring to sophisticated weaponry. . . What's missing, he adds, is the spark that will set events into motion. . . Over the course of my six weeks in Khartoum [the capital of Sudan], I came to understand bin Laden as a small part in a colossal machine that was growing day by day.

In 1996, the Sudanese government, under fierce international pressure, expelled bin Laden and later placed Turabi under house arrest. Bin Laden returned to Afghanistan, which was now ruled by the Taliban. After the 1998 bombings of U.S. embassies in Kenya and Tanzania, and the consequent public attention given to bin Laden by the U.S. government and the Western media, the persona of Osama bin Laden rocketed to mythic proportions among the world of frustrated Islamic peoples. Tall (6'5"), rugged, and articulate, he is the current figure of integration for the anti-civilization movement. More than just a leader, bin Laden is a cosmic symbol to all who are sold on the theological myth of the Islamic militant movement.

In the incisive *Rolling Stone* article by Michael Vlahos (November 8 issue), he further observes: "We also are fighting a new vision. Terrorism is just an expression of its tactics, and bin Laden—though an emotive mythic symbol—is ultimately just one *replicable leader* of a potentially vast following" (emphasis mine).

Under the current terms of engagement, the death of

bin Laden at the hands of America is likely to create ten replicas in his place. (This is by no means a suggestion that he should not be killed. The point is that the solution is on a scale vastly beyond the demise of bin Laden.)

Our own responsibility for the geopolitical conditions in which the terrorist movement developed is currently irrelevant. The broader issues need to be addressed in their own time, and such a time will require a serious searching of America's soul (although I am reasonably certain we will never do this). There are many related issues, but at the moment we do not have the luxury of adequately addressing those issues.

After we had delivered the Nazis and the children of Hirohito from the captivity of their own bloodthirsty madness, a relationship of mutual respect, friendship, and support developed among us. But so long as their armies were attempting to destroy us, we could not pursue the broader civilizational understandings and reconciliations.

The enemy we now confront is not as unique as the hype suggests. It has vulnerabilities that are easily accessible to us. The difficulty is not in locating the soft spot of this enemy, but rather in developing our awareness of the need to address the enemy at its weak and fatal point.

4.   Is Al Qaeda Really a Fringe Movement?

Al Qaeda is taking control of mainstream Islam outside of the West, in a fashion similar to the Nazi takeover of
German society in the early 1930s.

As a matter of political expediency, Western governments have sought to profile al Qaeda as a fringe movement.
This caricature has served a useful purpose for the U.S. and
British governments in their effort to stitch together a coalition that includes many nations with predominately Muslim
populations. President Bush and Prime Minister Blair have
made an extraordinary effort to explain to the world that we
are not at war with Islam, and that in fact we are a civilization of pluralistic societies inhabited by millions of Muslims
who are no less free than Christians, Jews, and Hindus to
observe their religion and express their love for it. This
emphasis by Western leaders has been crucial to the fledgling
success of governments in nations such as Jordan, Indonesia,
and Pakistan in rallying their people for support of the U.S.-
led "war on terrorism."
Politics is often a game of illusions, and its success
in this respect is contingent on the ability of the illusion to
present a more powerful appeal than the reality it seeks to
subdue. In this case, the illusion is the caricature of al
Qaeda as a fringe movement lacking widespread and overwhelming popular support in Islamic societies outside of the
West. The problem confronting this illusion is the impa-
tience and the intensifying fury of the reality it seeks to subdue. Fareed Zakaria is one of the analysts attempting to
sound the warning that we are dangerously ignoring the
empirical evidence that bin Laden and his colleagues are
heroes and icons for *many millions* of Middle Eastern and
Far Eastern Muslims. Mr. Zakaria observed in his Special
Report for the October 15 issue of *Newsweek:* "To say that

Al-Qaeda is a fringe group may be reassuring, but it is false. Read the Arab press in the aftermath of the attacks and you will detect a not-so-hidden admiration for bin Laden. . . The problem is not that Osama bin Laden believes that this is a religious war against America. It's that millions of people across the Islamic world seem to agree. . . In Iran, Egypt, Syria, Iraq, Jordan, the occupied territories and the Persian Gulf, the resurgence of Islamic fundamentalism is virulent, and a raw anti-Americanism seems to be everywhere. This is the land of suicide bombers, flag-burners and fiery mullahs."

The Economist, in its September 29 issue, reported that moderate Muslims in Pakistan are fearful of a societal and governmental takeover by the fundamentalists: "What westernized Pakistanis now fear is that the networks of armed Islamists have taken on a life of their own. One Lahore professor expects that he and his kind ['moderate' Muslims] will end up with their heads on pikes."

In the "Letters to the Editor" section of that same *Economist* issue, S. Shivasabesan of Canberra wrote: "Bombing Afghanistan, or any other [Muslim] country, will turn normal people into valuable new recruits to terrorism. All terrorist movements use violence as a strategy for they know that retaliation will bring new members into their fold. It is a win-win situation for them."

In an article for the October 25 issue of *Rolling Stone* magazine (which originally appeared in the June 25, 2000, issue of *New York Times Magazine*), Jeffrey Goldberg described his experience as a guest at the Haqqania religious school (madrasa) in Pakistan:

> Very few of the students at the Haqqania madrasa study anything but Islamic subjects. There are no world history courses, or math courses, or computer rooms or science labs at the

madrasa. The Haqqania madrasa is, in fact, a jihad factory.

This does not make it unique in Pakistan. There are one million students studying in the country's 10,000 or so madrasas, and militant Islam is at the core of most of these schools. . . Pakistan's Islamists are becoming more and more radicalized—"Talibanized," some call it—thanks in part to madrasas such as Haqqania, and Pakistan is showing early signs of coming apart at the seams. Pakistan also happens to be in possession of nuclear weapons. Many Muslim radicals say they believe these weapons should become part of the arsenal of jihad. It turns out that many of the Haqqania students, under careful tutelage, now believe it too.

Mr. Goldberg goes on to report how at one point he was allowed to directly address a class of madrasa students:

I began by saying that bin Laden's program violates a basic tenet of Islam, which holds that even in a jihad the lives of innocent people must be spared. A jihad is a war against combatants, not women and children. I read to them an appropriate saying of the Prophet Muhammad. . . It is narrated by Ibn Umar [the second successor, or *caliph,* to lead Islam after the death of Muhammad] that a woman was found killed in one of these battles, so the Messenger of Allah . . . forbade the killing of women and children.

They did not like the idea of me quoting the Prophet to them, and they began chanting, "Osama, Osama, Osama." When they calmed down, they took turns defending bin Laden.

"Osama bin Laden is a great Muslim," a student named Wali said. . .

I asked the students if they thought it would be permissible, by the law of Islam, to use a nuclear bomb during the prosecution of a jihad.

"All things come from Allah," a student said. "The atomic bomb comes from Allah, so it should be used."

I then asked: Who wants to see Osama bin Laden armed with nuclear weapons? Every hand in the room shot up.

After this encounter, Goldberg spoke individually with some of the students. He reports on his conversation with a young man named Sayid: "'How would [your parents] feel if you were killed [in the jihad]?' 'They would be very happy,' he said. 'They would be so proud. Any father would want his son to die as shaheed,' or martyr."

Goldberg later spoke with a seventeen-year-old fundamentalist named Muhammad, who told the reporter: "America is the place that wants to kill Osama. . . Osama is a great hero of the Muslims." Goldberg concludes his article by observing: "These are poor and impressionable boys kept entirely ignorant of the world. . . They are the perfect jihad machines."

These Islamic religious schools, the madrasas, have been churning out millions of angry, half-educated but heavily indoctrinated young men in countries from North Africa to the Indonesian archipelago. A majority of Muslims in these countries do not subscribe to this version of Islam, but they are a silent majority and they are rapidly losing the contest over who will control the definition and the destiny of Islam outside of the West. Fareed Zakaria observes in his *Newsweek* Special Report: "But as the moderate majority looks the other way, Islam is being taken over by a small poisonous element."

The historical parallels between the ascendancy of the Islamic terrorists and the rise of the Nazis cannot be overemphasized. When Hitler and his colleagues began their move to gain control of Germany, many millions of Germans did not subscribe to his doctrine or his vision. Yet by capitalizing on the discontent of the people (whose miserable living conditions were intensified by British, French, and U.S. post-War policies), by creating a concrete focus for their frustration and rage (the Jews and their supporters), and by presenting himself and the Nazi party as liberators with a workable vision of worldwide triumph for Germany, Hitler was able to win converts at an accelerating rate. As his movement gained momentum, those who disagreed with him became increasingly silent, or they left the country or were killed.

With few exceptions, the individual members of the Nazi Party were not insane, but the Nazi movement itself was. Those who joined the party and its cause were not necessarily evil within themselves, yet they had embraced a doctrine and a vision that is unconditionally evil. Of course there are important differences between the Nazis and the Islamic anti-civilization (the Nazi movement most likely would have collapsed, or at least fragmented, had Hitler been killed in the 1930s). Yet the historical parallels are both alarming and instructive. As with the Nazis, so with the Islamic terrorists—there can be no successful negotiations until they have already been destroyed. Being "nice" to them—offering financial assistance or promises of policy reform, or any other show of willingness to "work with them," will fuel their resolve to wage attacks against us, as any act of generosity on our part would be construed by them *only* as fear and weakness.

The goal of the terrorist movement is threefold.

It aims first of all to eradicate the Western presence

from the Middle East (meaning, in this respect, the Crescent from North Africa to Pakistan). It goes without saying that the first phase of this terrorist vision involves the overthrow of every non-fundamentalist government within the Crescent, and their replacement with a single, pan-Islamic government. (This would be on the model of the great Islamic caliphates of the past, and most emphatically from the seventh through eleventh centuries.)

The achievement of this first phase would lead immediately to a prosecution of the second, which is the annihilation of Israel. Even moderate Muslims throughout the Middle East are sympathetic to the idea of Israel's extinction. This passion for the death of "the Jew" and the burial of even the concept "Israel" is perhaps the most remarkable parallel to the macabre vision of the Nazis. The magnitude of this hatred of the Jews among the Muslims of the Middle East is difficult for us to grasp. No adequate reference for comparison exists anywhere within our own society. Although we are by no means strangers to group hatred—and in our own history we have engaged in revolting displays of group oppression and slaughter—there is no qualitative equivalent to the passionate thirst for Jewish blood that dominates the psychology of the Islamic peoples in the Middle East.

In summary, the first two phases of the terrorist vision are:

1) A withdrawal of all Western presence from the Middle East.
2) The extinction of Israel.

Yet even if these were granted (which they will never be), it would be understood by the fundamentalists as a stepping-stone to the third and final phase of their vision, which is the subjugation of the entire world to the new Caliphate. This, in a nutshell, is the mythic narrative embodied in Osama bin Laden and the many other heroes of the emerging Islamic mainstream in the Crescent.

We know their stated aims. We know the depth of their pledge to this vision. There can be no appeasement or any negotiation whatsoever.

Hitler also had some legitimate grievances. Those who attempted to negotiate with him in the early stages (such as Neville Chamberlain, the Prime Minister of England from 1937–40) are judged, by the general consensus of our civilization, as among the most repugnantly naïve and effete leaders in all of human history.

Although the religion of the mass murderers is not currently embraced by a majority of Middle Eastern Muslims, it has effectively seized control of the direction that Islam is taking in that part of the world.

Another example of the dwarfing of the majority by this ascending minority is chronicled by Fareed Zakaria in his account of an Egyptian sheik named Muhammad Rafaat Othman:

> Sheik Muhammad Rafaat Othman is a lonely man. Though he teaches Islamic law at the most prestigious Islamic school in the Middle East . . . he has no congregation to preach to. . . [He] is one of the few clerics in Egypt who insist that the Quran unconditionally bans suicide, even as a tactic in a legitimate holy war. "As I interpret our religion, I don't see any evidence of exceptions to this rule," he says. "You can expose yourself to a situation where you might get killed. But you can't knowingly take your life." That is not the only problem Sheik Muhammad sees with suicide bombings. "Attacking innocent, unarmed people is forbidden. Prophet Muhammad demanded that we

not kill women, children or the elderly. Attacks should be against soldiers and armed civilians." Sheik Muhammad is a rare voice of intellectual honesty in the Muslim clerical world. . .

[He] has searched the Quran and concluded that "there are no verses that say you can kill yourself—for any reason. Suicide attackers would say that this is the only way to serve Allah. But Allah does not ask you to do it." . . .

Sheik Muhammad says that he knows of *no other Islamic scholar in Egypt who shares his view*. And though he occasionally fills in as preacher for the imam in his village in the Nile delta, he doesn't seem to be getting the word out. (Emphasis mine)

Zakaria also reports:

Other clerics [outside of Egypt] have been occasionally brave enough to voice their doubts even about [Palestinian suicide bombers against Israel]. In May, the Grand Mufti of Saudi Arabia, Sheik Abdulaziz . . . told a newspaper: "Jihad for God's sake is one of the best acts of Islam, but killing yourself in the midst of the enemy, or suicidal acts, I don't know whether this is endorsed by Sharia . . . or whether it is considered jihad for God. I'm afraid it could be suicide." Clerics throughout the Middle East quickly dismissed his opinion or claimed he was quoted out of context.

Public support for the terrorists is escalating in such a way that the governments of Egypt, Saudi Arabia, and Pakistan are being pushed to the wall. The October 28 murder of fifteen Christians and a Muslim security guard at a church building in eastern Pakistan is a chilling exposure of the nature and momentum of the terrorist movement. The October 29 issue of the *Los Angeles Times* quoted an Islamabad professor, Rifaat Hussain: "[The slaughter of the fifteen Christians] is meant to show that the government is not in control and to say, 'If we can't kill Americans, we will kill Christians, the people of their faith.'"

The terrorists have no interest in the fact that many millions of Americans are not Christians, and that many Americans are in fact Muslims. It did not disturb the terrorists that these fifteen Christians, who were singing a hymn to God when the shooting began, were law-abiding Pakistani citizens. It did not disturb them that the security worker they killed was a Muslim, although the Koran promises eternal cursings and hell for anyone who kills a Muslim. In the logic of the terrorist movement, neither the Koran nor the empirical demographic facts of the world are allowed to interfere with their love of murder.

In a "Politics & People" article in the October 4 issue of the *Wall Street Journal,* Albert R. Hunt quotes a Ms. Julie Sirrs, who had conducted interviews in Yemen: "One Yemeni prisoner told me he would be willing to get on a school bus and kill children if the religious scholars told him to, even though he seemed aware that Islam did not condone the killing of innocents."

The slaughter of children is a particular pleasure for the Palestinian suicide bombers, who are heroes of immense status among a majority of the Palestinian people and throughout the Arab world. Until recently, we had watched such things from a distance.

Will we allow the vast and vulnerable homeland of America to also witness the massacre of our children coming home from school? The Palestinian suicide bombers envy and hate America no less fiercely than they do Israel. Their failure to duplicate within America what they are doing in Israel is due only to a current lack of opportunity. Will we wait for such barbaric developments within our homeland before we seriously consider raising the level of our strategy?

Al Qaeda is not a fringe group, but rather a symbol of the emerging mainstream of Islam outside of the West. Although it is not the majority (yet), the terrorist movement is in control of the direction and the definition of Islam beyond the West. A front-page article in the October 30 issue of the *Los Angeles Times* had the following sub-caption: "President [Musharraf] invites leaders of all major parties as mood of 'silent majority' shifts." The article went on to report: "The meetings come amid a discernible shift in the public mood in Pakistan in the last ten days, during which the government has sensed that mainstream opinion is beginning to turn against Musharraf's decision to back the bombing campaign. . . [Before the bombing began, Musharraf believed that] the extremists and fundamentalist religious parties . . . represent about 15% of the population. . . But the government's main concern now appears to be the far quieter shift it believes is underway within the vast "silent majority." . . . The normally fragmented religious parties have begun to show a more united front."

An important observation was made in the September 29 issue of *The Economist:* "In striking back at the terrorists . . . America has a dual aim: to stamp out the attackers, wherever they may be, and to deny them their goal of rallying Muslims to their cause." In response to this, I would suggest the following:

> 1) Our current effort at stamping out the ter-
> rorists in Afghanistan is creating multi-
> tudes of potential terrorists in other places
> (the slaughter of the fifteen Christians in
> Pakistan is a direct consequence of our

effort to stamp out the terrorists in Afghanistan).

2) Our current effort in Afghanistan is not hindering the terrorists' goal of rallying Muslims to their cause.

(In my insistence on such observations, I should not be misconstrued as seeking to slight the heroic activity and the formidable fighting capacity of our military people in Afghanistan. My point is that our current and valiant military effort in Central Asia is afflicting the body of our enemy but is not reaching to the generative level inside the enemy. Until we crush the terrorist movement *at this level,* we are chopping the viper without destroying the eggs it leaves behind.)

The Islamic terrorists are successfully profiling the conflict as a war of religions. Michael Vlahos concludes his article in the November 8 issue of *Rolling Stone* magazine with the following comment: "We want to fight our war, a 'war on terrorism.' But perhaps at last we will be forced to fight their war, a war of religion—not between classical faiths, perhaps, but between opposing visions of life and civilization."

The *Washington Post National Weekly Edition,* in its October 1 issue, described the massive terrorist plot that was exposed, and thereby aborted, by a freak accident in the Philippines in 1995:

> Arrested and tortured by Philippine intelligence agents in 1995, Abdul Hakim Murad told the story of "Bojinka" ("loud bang"), the code name bin Laden operatives had given to an audacious plan to bomb 11 U.S. airliners simultaneously and fly an airplane into the CIA

headquarters in Langley, Va.—all after attempting to assassinate Pope John Paul II. . . The plot in the Philippines . . . appears to be a model of the methods, aims and structure of the network that bin Laden's followers have assembled in dozens of countries around the world. . . Intelligence records indicate the precise flights that were to be targeted: United 808, Delta 59, Northwest 6, and others. . . The plotters also included in their plans the motives for the mission, in a manifesto recovered by investigators: "The U.S. government gives military aircraft to the Jewish state. . . All people who support the U.S. government are our target."

The terrorists, who are religiously committed to the wholesale extinction of the Jewish state, view the U.S. government as symbiotically related to the Jewish state. Their hatred of Americans has ballooned into an identity equivalent of their hatred of Israeli Jews.

The *Post* article explains how the terrorists planned to murder the pope: "One of them would hide [the bomb] under a priest's robes, and try to get close enough to kiss the pontiff as the bomb went off."

The terrorists do not distinguish between Protestant and Catholic, just as Christians in general do not distinguish between Shiite and Sunni Muslims. (The fifteen Christians killed in Pakistan were Protestants worshipping in a Catholic building, for want of another building to gather in.) In the assessment of the terrorists, the pope is the supreme visible symbol of Christianity. In their thinking, to assassinate the pope would not only be a devastating blow to "Christian civilization," but also an act that would spark hostilities between Islamic and Christian peoples throughout the world. Furthermore, Pope John Paul II is a particular threat to the terrorist movement on account of his strenuous efforts to relieve the historic tensions between Islam and Christianity. The terrorists who are taking control of Islam need the Muslims in their part of the world to perceive Christians as collaborators with Jews in a sophisticated conspiracy to destroy Islam. In their profiling of the conflict as a war of religions, the terrorists feel their cause is threatened by a pope who reaches out with a generous and friendly hand to the Muslim world. Their plot to kill Pope John Paul II had a two-field aim of eliminating this threat and sparking a civilizational confrontation.

The terrorists do not want peace. Nothing we can say or do will appease them. They want only two things, neither of which we will ever give them: the extinction of Israel, and a single Caliphate imposing Sharia on the entire world.

Christianity, "the West," and the Jews form an existential synthesis in the worldview of the terrorists and their supporters. They have pledged themselves and the name of their god to the extinction of this perceived synthesis. No Christian, no Westerner, and no Jew will be safe until the Islamic militant movement is obliterated at its generative source.

"The enemy lives in a world of myths and heroes," Michael Vlahos noted in his article for the November 8 issue of *Rolling Stone*. This was exemplified in the words of bin Laden himself, in a speech after several Pakistani Taliban supporters had been killed during demonstrations in Karachi:

> I received with great sorrow the news of the murder of some of our Muslim brothers in Karachi while they were expressing their opposition to the American crusade forces and their allies on the lands of Muslims in Pakistan and Afghanistan. We ask Allah to accept them as martyrs and include

them with prophets. . . Whoever of them left children behind, they are my children, and I am their caretaker, Allah willing. . . We hope that these brothers are among the first martyrs in Islam's battle in this era against the new Christian-Jewish crusade led by the big crusader Bush under the flag of the Cross; this battle is considered one of Islam's battles. . .We incite our Muslim brothers in Pakistan to give everything they own and are capable of to push the American crusade forces from invading Pakistan and Afghanistan. The Prophet . . . said: Whoever didn't fight, or prepare a fighter, or take good care of a fighter's family, Allah will strike him with a catastrophe before Judgment Day. (Quoted from the *Los Angeles Times,* September 25 issue)

America and its allies have been assaulted by a new vision of possibilities—a new vision of God, of human nature, and of the future of the world. This vision is unequivocally evil, and it presents a threat to us no less venomous than that posed by the Nazis sixty years ago. The biggest mistake of that "Greatest Generation" was in nearly waiting too long before unleashing its total destructive capacity against the Nazi regime. Our delay in deciding to crush Hitler almost gave him the time he needed to develop an atomic bomb. We should consider the potential consequences of delaying our implementation of a dramatically intensified strategy that would promise to swiftly crush the spirit of al Qaeda and restore to our society the sense of security we have allowed our children to lose.

A dangerous problem for America is that many among us do not understand violence. It is an elementary reality in the real world of human beings. It is a frightening and revolting thing, yet a paradox of violence is that it can be overcome only by a confrontation with itself. The love of violence is not overcome by demonstrations of kindness. Only by an overwhelming display of controlled violence is the reckless love of violence crushed. Our only hope of eliminating the self-replicating Islamic terrorist movement is to calmly raise the magnitude of aggressive strategy beyond anything the terrorists and their supporters have ever imagined.

5.   Re-Evaluating Our Self-Imposed Restrictions

After September 11, we pummeled ourselves for our lack of preparedness against what is assaulting us. It is true that we are unprepared for many things. Yet we are well prepared to do the most urgent thing.

Although our air and ground forces are superior to anything al Qaeda could mount against us, there are no conceivable means of plugging all the holes through which the terrorists can reach and draw blood. Bin Laden himself boasted after the September 11 mass-destruction attacks: "There is America, hit by God in one of its softest spots."

If the extent of our country and our interests were the size of Catalina Island, we could likely develop a shield for all the "soft spots." But our land is vast and our people have interests throughout the world, as abu Ghaith taunted: "The American interests are everywhere, all over the world."

Since September 11, we have magnified our security efforts at an enormous financial cost, and yet every hour we anxiously wonder what the next newscast might report. How long will we *impose upon ourselves* the need to live with such anxiety?

We possess capacities that al Qaeda is presuming we will never introduce. Al Qaeda is predicating all things, even the conditions of its own existence, on our self-imposed bondage to the more restrictive interpretations of our national philosophy. In this clash of Western idealism against an anti-civilizational realism, we have placed ourselves at a disadvantage of our own making.

The terrorists have shown not only a willingness to kill indiscriminately, but also a relish in doing so. As in Kenya and Tanzania, so also in New York City—al Qaeda murdered children, women, and men; black, brown, and white; Muslim, Christian, Hindu, and Jew. The Koran forbids suicide, and it forbids the deliberate killing of women and children. Even more ironic, in verse 93 of chapter five, it reads: "If a man kills a believer [that is, a Muslim] intentionally, his recompense is Hell, to abide therein: and the wrath and the curse of Allah are upon him, and a dreadful chastisement is prepared for him."

Muslims from more than ten different countries were killed in the Trade Center, along with thousands of women. *According to the Koran,* those terrorists are in Hell under the everlasting curse of Allah. Yet they were persuaded by their religious leaders of a place in Paradise with an eternity of good sex. The realism of the Islamic fundamentalists is so complete that the Koran itself is not permitted to interfere with their erotic obsession about death.

A poster boy for the militant movement is Mohammed Atta, who came from Egypt and lived for years off the comfort and hospitality of our land. He was free to attend our mosques, to eat in our restaurants, to learn in our schools (he chose an aviation school), and to earn good money in jobs even while many Americans remained unemployed. In return for our generosity, Atta, the leader of the cell of terrorists in the September 11 attacks, slaughtered thousands of our people along with many guests from other nations.

In the property that Atta left behind, prayers were found that were written under the heading "The Last Night." These prayers were obviously for recitation by Atta and the other suicide hijackers during the night prior to their deeds. The prayers read, in part: "I pray to you God . . . to allow me to glorify you in every possible way. . . Oh God, open all doors for me. Oh God, who answers prayers and answers those who ask you, I am asking you for help. . . I am asking you to lift the burden I feel. Oh God, you who open all doors, please open all doors for me, open all venues for me, open all avenues for me" (quoted from the *Los Angeles*

Times, September 28).

Other writings under "The Last Night" spoke encouragingly of soon being with "the women of Paradise": "And know that the Gardens of Paradise are beautified with its best ornaments, and its inhabitants are calling you. And if . . . you kill, then kill completely, because this is the way of the Chosen One."

Atta sought to glorify his god by incinerating thousands of people who had done him no wrong in a country that had offered him its best. He believed his reward for this was an eternity in Paradise with exotically beautiful women serving his passions forever. The culture of the militants is such that it produces its heroes in the mold of mass murderers such as Mohammed Atta. Hundreds of thousands, perhaps millions, of young Muslims aspire to the civilizational fame and erotic reward pursued by Atta. Our controlling moral imperative today is to articulate and prosecute a strategy that would promise to rapidly obliterate the psychological structure of the Islamic militant movement. Hard punches to the body alone will not accomplish this. A decisive solution will be reached only by an aggressive penetration to the soul (without leaving the rest undone).

We can reasonably assume that one of the more immediate objectives of al Qaeda this moment is a seizure of the nuclear arsenal in Pakistan. L. Paul Bremer III, a former chairman of the National Commission on Terrorism, was asked by Paul Alexander in an interview for *Rolling Stone* magazine: "What are other possible domino effects of a U.S. military action [in Afghanistan]?" After expressing concern about instability in Saudi Arabia, Bremer spoke of the situation in Pakistan: "Pakistan is in a very difficult position. . . There could be a coup."

That is a disturbing response to a question of incalculable importance. Michael Vlahos responded to the same question in the following way: "If the regime in Pakistan fell and was replaced by Islamicist elements, that would mark a new stage in the conflict and a sobering escalation. If that were to happen, we'd have to make a major effort to go in and get their nuclear weapons or destroy them."

In all likelihood, in such a situation we would be unable to capture or destroy the nuclear arsenal without first destroying the governing body in Pakistan, and possibly a considerable portion of the country itself. If militant fundamentalists succeed in taking control of Pakistan's nuclear weapons, which is all too conceivable of a possibility, we will have already waited too long. If the militants were to seize control of Pakistan, a nuclear attack to eliminate a new threat to us would raise the cost of human life into the millions, perhaps even the tens of millions. The situation is not yet completely out of control, but it is held together only by a thread.

It is true that we cannot seamlessly defend even a majority of our "soft spots," but an offensive strategy of overwhelming intensity would show the supporters of terrorism that the cost of afflicting America with deadly assaults is *far too high.* Al Qaeda is banking on our idealism and using it against us in a chilling dance of cultural judo. Since the breadth of our geographical presence makes us acutely vulnerable, and since the terrorists are not intimated by the present magnitude of our military response, we should re-evaluate the restrictions we have placed upon ourselves.

The means of destroying this enemy is within our grasp. All that restrains us from eliminating the Islamic terrorist movement is our hitherto lack of willingness to articulate and prosecute the necessary strategy.

Part Three:

A New Architecture

6.　Resurrecting the Myth of Superpower

Osama bin Laden boasted that the "myth of superpower" died in his imagination, and in the imagination of Muslims throughout the Middle East, when the Soviet Union was compelled by the mujahedin to retreat from Afghanistan. It is in our interest to resurrect what died in their minds.

In a stirring article for the November 3 issue of *The Economist,* Graham Allison, author and former assistant secretary of defense, noted: "In a 1997 CNN interview, [bin Laden boasted that] 'the myth of the superpower was destroyed not only in my mind, but also in the minds of all Muslims,' when the mujahideen defeated the Russians in Afghanistan. In his view . . . the United States—as seen in its withdrawal from Lebanon in 1983 after the deaths of 241 marines, and its precipitous retreat from Somalia in 1993 after 18 special-forces soldiers died—is cowardly."

Bin Laden conveniently fails to factor some relevant variables into his logic, such as the crucial support that the mujahedin received from the United States during that ten-year war. But most emphatically, bin Laden and his tens of thousands of colleagues have evolved a remarkable psychology of denial concerning the true military capacity of the Soviet Union. The Soviets, if they had only willed to do so, could have turned Afghanistan into a sea of fire. If the Soviets had done so, bin Laden and his fellow mujahedin would have been left with nothing for their families to bury. Even their bones would not have survived a genuine expression of the military capacity of a "superpower." There is a single reason why the Soviets did not use their ultimate weapons to destroy the mujahedin: the superpower supporting the mujahedin. A Soviet strike with nuclear weapons anywhere on earth during the Cold War era would likely have resulted in a direct conflict with the U.S. (and possibly also with China).

A similar restraint was imposed on the United States when it faced the potential threat of an attack with chemical and biological weapons by the Iraqis during the Gulf War. After serious debate among his senior civilian and military advisors, President George Bush decided the U.S. would *not* use nuclear weapons in such an event. Although the Berlin Wall had come down and the Cold War was widely touted as being "over," the Soviet Union still existed and was providing considerable military support to Saddam Hussein. The Soviet Union also remained a highly suspicious archenemy of the United States. The use of nuclear weapons by the U.S. in Iraq, or even the threat of a nuclear strike, would have mobilized the hard-liners among the Soviets and possibly led to a reversal in the declining Russian will to sustain a totalitarian ideology in lethal conflict with the U.S.-led free world. The U.S. government could not have used nuclear weapons in Iraq for the same reasons the Soviet Union did not use them in Afghanistan. The Cold War realities were a boon to both the mujahedin and Saddam Hussein.

Osama bin Laden and his colleagues, and their millions of supporters throughout the Middle East, have failed to process the logic that prevented the Soviet Union from completely annihilating the mujahedin. This failure of intelligence on the part of the Islamic fundamentalists resulted in bin Laden's boast that "the myth of the superpower was destroyed not only in my mind, but also in the minds of all Muslims." In all truth, the Soviets lost to the mujahedin because their regard for the power of the United States prevented them from using the weapons that would have liquidated the mujahedin. Bin Laden and his friends have left a very important detail out of their reasoning.

This misconception, widespread among the Islamic nations, is a principal motivating delusion for the terrorists and their supporters. The misinterpretation of the mujahedin victory in Afghanistan has served as an intoxicant, fueling the idea that radicalized and militant Islam is capable of conquering the governments of the Middle East, the civilization led by America, and eventually the entire world. The results of the 1989 Soviet withdrawal on the psychology of the mujahedin are well summarized in an article by Yaroslav Trofimov in the November 16 issue of the *Wall Street Journal:* "Returning Afghan veterans such as Mr. bin Laden have helped destabilize much of the Arab world, fueling terrorist groups such as Egypt's Islamic Jihad, Algeria's GIA and the Aden Abyan Islamic Army in Yemen. *Intoxicated with their success in defeating a superpower,* many of these returning fighters have shown little respect for the rulers of their own countries, accusing them of failing to uphold Islamic values and of collaborating with the U.S. Some proceeded to kill government officials and Western tourists" (emphasis mine).

"Intoxicated with their success in defeating a superpower." The Soviet withdrawal has created a madness that can be cured only by an overwhelming display of superpower capacity and intent.

As I write (November 23), America is experiencing a groundswell of optimism over the stunning collapse of the Taliban positions throughout Afghanistan. We have no confirmed al Qaeda-sponsored terrorist attacks on our soil since the bombing began. Public demonstrations against America in Islamic nations have declined in number and intensity, and the Afghan people are celebrating over the dead bodies of Arabs and Pakistanis as the Taliban remnants flee with the al Qaeda remnants to their southern mountain strongholds. This is being heralded as a decisive psychological defeat for the terrorist mass movement, and also as evidence that there is actually very little support for radical Islam in the Muslim countries. Even Fareed Zakaria, whom I previously quoted as insisting that al Qaeda is not a fringe movement, now seems to be of a different opinion. He writes in the November 26 issue of *Newsweek:* "Now we need to spread the cheer. The American position in the Arab world—particularly among its leaders—is stronger than it has been in years. Victory does that. . . We should say to the leaders of Egypt, Saudi Arabia and the rest: 'The past two months have shown that there is no tidal wave of fundamentalism in your lands. . .' Osama bin Laden did seem to appeal to millions of frustrated people in the Islamic world. But much of his appeal was as an alternative to the wretched regimes of the Arab world and as a symbol of defiance against the mighty American superpower. Once you take success away from bin Laden, what's left is a spoiled Saudi millionaire with a medieval world view. It turned out there wasn't much support for that in the Muslim world."

It is my hope that Zakaria is correct. But I struggle with disturbing doubts.

As to the decrease in anti-American demonstrations among the Islamic nations, we should consider that the governments of those nations have taken extreme measures to accomplish this. If many of the key agitators in those countries have been arrested (or detained), and if the governments have effectively served notice that demonstrations will be closely monitored by heavily armed police on the lookout for expressions of radicalism, it is difficult to infer from the decreased number of demonstrations that "the past two months have shown that there is no tidal wave of fundamentalism in your lands." It is difficult to infer that "the American position in the Arab world . . . is stronger than it has been in years." Among the corrupt and intimidated Arab governments, yes. But among the oppressed, frustrated, and heavily indoctrinated masses?

Perhaps time will show that Zakaria is correct, but I am inclined to suspect the pressures of the times have induced him into a leap of wishful thinking (or into a capitulation to pop journalism).

In his saying, "it turns out that there wasn't much support for [bin Laden's doctrine] in the Muslim world," Zakaria has repudiated his seemingly well-studied observation of six weeks ago: "To say that Al-Qaeda is a fringe group may be reassuring, but it is false. Read the Arab press in the aftermath of the attacks and you will detect a not-so-hidden admiration for bin Laden. . . The problem is not that Osama bin Laden believes that this is a religious war against America. It's that millions of people across the Islamic world seem to agree. . . In Iran, Egypt, Syria, Iraq, Jordan, the occupied territories and the Persian Gulf, the resurgence of Islamic fundamentalism is virulent, and a raw anti-Americanism seems to be everywhere."

Which of these Fareed Zakarias has done his proper homework?

Because the repressive measures of brutal, U.S.-supported Arab governments have dampened the public expressions of anti-American fury, should we conclude with the new Zakaria, "the American position in the Arab world . . . is stronger than it has been in years"? Or that "it turns out there wasn't much support for [fundamentalism] in the Muslim world"? Granted, it would temporarily make us feel better if we could believe such things. That is until the next shocking terrorist act insults our wishful thinking and once again we watch the Arabs dancing in the streets.

We should also consider that Mohammed Omar recently dissuaded many wannabe jihad warriors from coming to Afghanistan to fight with the Taliban. As the Taliban positions were collapsing under the stampede of American bombs and Northern Alliance fighters, Omar, the Taliban leader, dispatched instructions to militant supporters in other countries: "Save your life, go to your homes, but keep your arms underground. At the moment we have no need of Taliban because they are bombing us, but after some time if we need help from you, we will find you through your

party" (quoted from the *Los Angeles Times,* November 15).
The word has gone out from the Taliban high command: "Lie low."

Omar did not instruct his supporters throughout the world to repent and conform to a more civilized version of Islam. He instructed them to *lie low until an opportune time.*

George F. Will has recently warned, "Now there is a danger of . . . thinking that the war on terrorism is now a mere mopping-up operation" (*Newsweek,* November 26). In that same article, Will goes on to report: "In Germany last week, in an unusual public meeting of senior officials from German and U.S. investigative and intelligence agencies, [it was made known] that *at least 70,000* Islamic fundamentalists have passed through Al-Qaeda's terrorist-training camps in the last few years. And Michael Rolince, head of the FBI's antiterrorism section, warned, 'These people do not retire. We will find them, or we will hear from them again'" (emphasis mine).

We can only hope that the rapid advances in Afghanistan have uncovered lists of names and mentions of plans.

The *Los Angeles Times* reported in its November 19 issue:

> "Sleeper" terrorists in position before Sept. 11 could be planning attacks against Western interests in general and U.S. targets in particular. . . A pan-Islamic legion of thousands has trained in the now-devastated Al Qaeda camps in Afghanistan and operate underground throughout Europe. . . "They have succeeded in creating a very motivated core that is present everywhere," said Alain Grignard, a Belgian expert on Islamic terrorism. . . New arrests in Spain and France have contributed to a picture

of an interconnected network of cells that
reaches into Britain, Italy, Belgium, Germany
and the Netherlands. . . The ultimate fear of
investigators in Europe is that an already
entrenched team of the caliber of the Sept. 11
hijackers is preparing a devastating attack or
series of strikes.

An alarming feature of the al Qaeda method is its
careful and long-term planning. The *Times* article continues: "A report issued Wednesday by the British government
warned: 'Based on our experience of the way the network
has operated in the past, other cells, like those that carried
out the terrorist attacks on 11 September, must be assumed
to exist.' There are indications that 'two or three' major
plots were set in motion before the hijack attacks in the
United States and that they could be well underway, a
European intelligence source said. 'I think Al Qaeda operations are in a real advanced state of planning,' the intelligence source said. 'Osama bin Laden follows a plan along
a certain timeline, going step by step, and the next step was
planned long ago.'"

Graham Allison, in his compelling article in the
November 3 *Economist,* wrote: "In contrast [with the U.S.
government's lack of preparedness], Mr. bin Laden and his
al Qaeda network have been thinking, planning and training
for this war for most of a decade." Allison also quotes bin
Laden from his 1997 CNN interview: "The nature of the battle requires good preparation."

The point should be emphasized that bin Laden gave
this statement about "good preparation" *four years ago.* The
planning, as I have noted earlier in this essay, has been
developing on an ambitious and comprehensive scale since
the early 1990s in Sudan (as was well known by the U.S.
intelligence community and the political leadership).

Near the end of 1996, presidential advisor Dick Morris assured Charlie Rose that one of Mr. Clinton's main goals for 1997 was to "crush terrorism." When this did not happen, even after such an assurance from a top advisor to the President of the United States, the terrorist movement was handed yet another boost to its inflated psychology. It had defeated the Soviet Union, murdered hundreds of U.S. Marines in Lebanon and Somalia, been exposed in a plot to blow up eleven U.S. airliners, and suffered no significant retaliation from the U.S. Its heart grew larger with each new success. Then Dick Morris announced the president's goal of crushing terrorism in 1997, and the threat was exposed by time as a puff of words. Rather than seeing an onslaught of U.S. power against them in 1997, the terrorists were treated to pictures of Dick Morris sucking the toes of a prostitute, and of a blue dress with the stain of a distracted and double-speaking president.

The movement rolled on, training by day, and planning by night. It felt itself unstoppable, invincible, and incapable of failure. As the bombs now rain down on Afghanistan, Omar holds fast to the Terrorist Confession: "The real matter is the extinction of America."

The *Times* reported in its November 16 issue: "Even as the Taliban appeared to be severely weakened and on the run, supreme leader Mullah Mohammed Omar warned Wednesday of the imminent demolition of the United States. 'The current situation of Afghanistan is related to a big cause—that is, the destruction of America,' Omar told BBC radio's Pushtun-language service. 'We will see this in a short time.' Asked whether a concrete plan for such destruction existed, Omar replied: 'The plan is going ahead, and, God willing, it is being implemented. But it is a huge task which is beyond the will and comprehension of human beings. If God's help is with us, this will happen within a short period of time. Keep in mind this prediction.'"

Is Omar bluffing, or is something in the works that is "beyond the comprehension" of us all? What was to happen on September 11 was "beyond the comprehension" of nearly all of us. The terrorists have already stated and shown the magnitude of their ambition and their gall. And over *70,000* of them have trained for death and destruction in recent years. It is very likely that Omar *is* bluffing, and also that Osama was bluffing when he recently claimed to have nuclear weapons. But why should we wait to respond proportionately, when there is even a small chance that Omar and Osama are *not* bluffing?

Our only safe assumptions are that many terrorist cells are waiting in the wings, that a catastrophic series of attacks are in the advanced stage of preparation, and that many millions of terrorist supporters and sympathizers in the Crescent are lying low under orders from their religious leaders and under the threatening posture of their governments. Our only safe response is a preemptive measure that will overwhelm the psychology of the terrorist movement and its widespread support base.

A solemn lesson in the capacity-differential between a team of superpowers and a network of angry criminals is the order of the day. Bin Laden has attested that the Soviet withdrawal "destroyed the myth of the superpower" in the minds of the fundamentalists. It is in our interest, and it is within our means, to swiftly restore this myth.

The psychology of the terrorists and their supporters is such that they are absolutely convinced we will grow weary and, eventually, back off. We have given them reasons for believing this, and there is no cure for their current madness other than a corrective expression of superpower capacity.

Ho Chi Minh warned the French, and then the Americans: "For every ten of us you kill, we will kill one of you. And in the end, you will grow tired." Had we only willed to do so, we could have destroyed Ho Chi Minh with measures beyond his ability to resist. But we were prevented in principle from doing so because of Cold War realities. Our answer was to sacrifice 50,000 of our people and 600,000 of theirs in a war that threatened to drag on forever, and during which time our government leaders "attended the truth with a bodyguard of lies." But when we left the land of Ho Chi Minh, his people did not come after us. The enemy we now confront *has* come after us, and we can only assume *he is continuing* to come after us. Since we have a capacity that can alter the psychology of this enemy, why are we fighting *in a manner that does not intimidate him?*

7.   Proliferation is Non-Containable Within the Present Order

Within the parameters of the present world order, the proliferation of weapons of mass destruction is *inevitable*. It can be slowed down, but ultimately it is *non-containable*. This process can be reversed only by means of an entirely new architecture.

Several years ago, the assistant secretary of defense under President Clinton warned: "Absent a major new initiative, we have every reason to expect there will be an act of nuclear terrorism in the next decade, maybe sooner." No "major new initiative" was launched, and the clock continues ticking. Bin Laden announced on Christmas Eve of 1998: "If I seek to acquire such weapons [nuclear and chemical], this is a religious duty. How we use them is up to us" (quoted by the *Los Angeles Times,* November 7). The *Times* article also reports: "In a federal court earlier this year, a former Bin Laden aide testified that he had tried to obtain weapons-grade uranium offered by a former Sudanese government minister. He paid $1.5 million for a 'heavy, shielded cylinder' purportedly containing enriched uranium and received a $10,000 cash bonus from Al Qaeda, he testified. But he said he didn't know whether the cylinder actually contained uranium—or whether it eventually made it to Al Qaeda."

It is no longer a secret that a considerable amount of weapons-grade uranium and plutonium, manufactured in the Soviet Union, is now unaccounted for. Since 1993, there have been over 175 known cases of trafficking in nuclear materials. The *Times'* article goes on to report: "The international Atomic Energy Agency . . . has recorded 175 cases of trafficking in nuclear materials since 1993. It has recorded 18 cases involving small amounts of highly enriched uranium or plutonium, the material needed to make a nuclear bomb. . . Short of making a nuclear bomb, agency experts say, terrorists could attach radioactive waste to a conventional bomb, spreading the waste. . . Bin Laden's interest in obtaining nuclear, biological or chemical weapons has worried U.S. counterterrorism authorities for years, a Bush administration official said. . . 'It has become clear that these guys have been very interested in acquiring these kinds of capabilities,' said the official, who asked not to be identified. 'Whether they have [obtained these capabilities] or not is not clear.'"

Our government leaders have been well aware of this emerging threat for quite some time. In the October 15 issue of the *Washington Post Weekly,* in a book review by Mark Bowden on David Halberstam's *War in a Time of Peace,* he observes: "One of the most important questions we face is why we delayed for so long taking strong preemptive action."

U.S. taxpayers fork over a trillion dollars a year to fund the operations of the U.S. government. Hundreds of billions of these dollars are spent on security-related issues. The taxpayers and their children have trusted that the government is responsibly using its well-funded capacity to protect our nation from threats of this magnitude. Graham Allison, the former Assistant Secretary of Defense previously quoted, also wrote in his article for the November 3 issue of *The Economist:* "Yet as the American government scrambles to pursue a war for which it had not prepared . . . it gallops off in all directions. It does so without a comprehensive assessment of the threats it now faces, and lacking a coherent strategy for combating mega-terrorism. . . Just a year ago the FBI had assured the administration that it had a "handle" on all al-Qaeda operatives within the United States."

Mr. Allison also reports on the findings of a bipartisan task-force led by former Senate Majority Leader Howard Baker, who presented the findings to the Bush administration in January: "The principal finding of the task-force is that '*the most urgent unmet national security threat to the United States today* is the danger that weapons of mass destruction or weapons-usable material in Russia could be stolen, sold to terrorists or hostile nation-states, and used against American troops abroad or citizens at home.' . . As Mr. Baker testified to the Senate Foreign Relations Committee in March, 'It really boggles my mind that there could be 40,000 nuclear weapons, or maybe 80,000 in the former Soviet Union, poorly controlled and poorly stored, and that the world isn't in a near state of hysteria about the danger'" (emphasis Allison's).

We should keep in mind that these are not the rantings of a half-educated and sparsely informed fanatic. Howard Baker was the leader of the United States Senate. The challenging words of Mark Bowden are worth repeating: "One of the most important questions we face are why we delayed for so long taking strong preemptive action."

In Allison's November 3 *Economist* article, he also reminded us: "A few years ago Boris Yeltsin's assistant for national security affairs, Alexander Lebed, reported that 40 out of 100 special KGB suitcase nuclear weapons were not accounted for in Russia. Under pressure from colleagues, he later retreated to the official Russian line that all nuclear weapons are secure and accounted for, but his twists and turns left more questions than answers."

The *Los Angeles Times* reported on November 7: "In recent weeks, Russian media have reported that Bin Laden has bought several suitcase-size nuclear bombs from Russia that have not been used only because they are protected by Soviet codes requiring a signal from Moscow before they can be detonated."

It is a reasonable certainty that this report in the Russian media is a wild rumor. But the warning of Lebed is a cause for great concern. Lebed was a high-ranking general and the director for Russian national security affairs. If the suitcase nuclear weapons were missing, he would be one of the few who would certainly have known about it. Lebed also at that time was hoping to become the next president of Russia. Can we suppose he would have compromised his career by issuing a bogus warning of such terrifying magnitude? Perhaps he would have and did. Only one thing for us is certain: we do not know.

Allison also observes: "Thanks to extraordinary professionalism on the part of Russian military and security guards, many attempts to steal weapons have been thwarted. . . The American government knows of no case at present in which those who wish to make nuclear weapons have acquired either the weapon, or sufficient nuclear materials to make one. What must worry us, however, is *what we don't know*" (emphasis mine).

Allison's point about the danger of "what we don't know" is all the more magnified when we recall that, "Just a year ago the FBI had assured the administration that it had a 'handle' on all al-Qaeda operatives within the United States." Allison warns what could happen even with a crude nuclear device: "Even a crude nuclear device could create an explosive force of 10,000 to 20,000 tons of TNT, demolishing an area of about three square miles. Not only the World Trade Centre, but also all of Wall Street and the financial district, and the lower tip of Manhattan up to Gramercy Park, would have disappeared. Hundreds of thousands of people would have died suddenly."

Brent Scowcroft and Daniel Poneman wrote in the October 31 issue of the *Los Angeles Times:* "A plutonium ingot the size of a soda can could fuel a nuclear explosion that could kill 50,000 people."

Allison continues in his *Economist* article: "Even an assembled device, like a suitcase nuclear weapon, could be shipped in a container, in the hull of a ship, or in a trunk carried by an aircraft. After September 11th, the number of containers that are X-rayed has increased to approximately 10%: 500 of the 5,000 containers currently arriving daily at the port of New York/New Jersey. But as the chief executive of CSX Lines, one of the foremost container-shipping companies, put it: 'If you can smuggle heroin in containers, you may be able to smuggle in a nuclear bomb.'"

Should we dismiss Allison, Scowcroft, and Baker as alarmists, along with the many other highly credentialed and informed persons who have attempted for years to persuade our government to take aggressive preemptive measures against this threat? Or should we give urgent heed to the repeated warnings of these informed individuals, and support our government in taking immediate and, if necessary, ultimate measures to strike at the root of this threat?

The genie is out of the bottle. The know-how and the wherewithal for building nuclear bombs are proliferating and, although it can be slowed down, ultimately it cannot be contained. The material for building crude nuclear bombs is out there, along with the know-how. As this threat has developed, our government has not responded with adequate preemptive measures because it could not be made to believe *the will to do it* is also out there. Today we have no excuse for such naïveté. It is unlikely that the terrorists have obtained nuclear weapons. But it is very likely that the terrorists have obtained radioactive materials capable of accomplishing horrific destructions in America and Europe. If they do not have these materials now, it is a virtual one hundred percent certainty that, *eventually,* unless a paradigmatically new architecture is imposed on the world, the proliferation of materials and know-how will consummate in a spectacular nuclear strike by a terrorist.

Such weapons could be smuggled into our country piece by piece. In the basement of a mosque they could be assembled and carried to various locations throughout the country. In the light of what we know today, it cannot be denied that the following hypothetical scenario, or something of similar magnitude, could become a reality in the very near future: "Two small nuclear bombs are simultaneously detonated in non-populous regions within the U.S. homeland. Minutes before the blasts, key government leaders and media personalities are contacted and notified of what is about to occur, and of who is responsible for it. Immediately following the blasts, the U.S. is notified by the responsible party that suicide bombers, each armed with a small nuclear weapon capable of destroying all life and property within a three-mile radius, are positioned in fifteen of the most heavily populated and commercially important areas of the United States. The demands of the responsible party are. . ."

If we wait for *some such scenario* to develop, it is certain to develop. We should recall the urgent summons of former U.S. Senate Majority Leader Howard Baker: "It really boggles my mind that there could be 40,000 nuclear weapons, or maybe 80,000 in the former Soviet Union, poorly controlled and poorly stored, and that the world isn't in a state of near hysteria about the danger."

Denial and wishful thinking will not cause this danger to diminish or disappear. (Our government leadership had evidently experimented with that method throughout the 1990s. President Bush's recent public disclosure and warning of the nuclear danger is news to most of the American public, but this is not new information to the U.S. intelligence community or to the political leadership.) Neither will our decisive battlefield victories in Afghanistan serve as an effective deterrent to the nuclear, chemical, and biological danger.

I am hardly suggesting our military effort in Afghanistan is not crucial to our national security interests and to world stability. Our current effort in Afghanistan is imperative to the overall war effort, but it will not prove to be the decisive measure in our eventual success against the terrorists.

There is no question as to the eventual and complete success of our military effort in Central Asia, as I stated earlier: "We have clearly weakened the Taliban's military capabilities, and the Special Forces being sent in are the most formidable fighting teams in the world. There is no question that our soldiers on the ground will destroy the Taliban positions wherever they find them." I also stated in that passage (written during the first week in November): "Yet by every indication, our campaign in Afghanistan is incubating further threats against us, and will continue to do so even after we have completely destroyed the Taliban."

Less than two weeks after that passage was written, the Taliban was fleeing in disarray. It is natural and proper for us to feel some measure of jubilation over our military's success against such a perverse enemy. But can we honestly say we now feel safer? Gerald F. Seib wrote for the *Wall Street Journal* on November 14: "Even at this hour of success, though, it's worth bearing in mind a more troubling long-term problem. In brief, it is this: The broader Islamic world will remain a veritable *incubator of more Osamas* if today's trends aren't reversed. . . There are hundreds of millions of young Muslims out there: even if Osama bin Laden goes away, they won't" (emphasis mine).

A previously mentioned article in that same *Journal* issue reported: "Tom Ridge and . . . Donald Rumsfeld both warned that the crumbling of Afghanistan's ruling Taliban could lead to new attacks in the U.S. Mr. Ridge said other terrorists are 'waiting in the wings' to replace Osama bin Laden if he is captured or killed.'"

The effective deterrent will not be the capture or death of bin Laden, or promises to the Muslim nations that we will take an active interest in their welfare. Neither the bombs nor the care packages dropped in Afghanistan have, in any significant measure, altered the psychology of the terrorists and their support base. They remain absolutely convinced that their god will bless their persistence in this worldwide campaign of terror, and that they will wear out the United States just as the Vietcong wore us out and just as the mujahedin wore out the Soviets (despite massive bombing campaigns in both wars). It is true that our aggression and triumphs in Afghanistan are causing great concern for terrorist-harboring governments throughout the Middle East. But these governments are hated by their most vocal citizens, and these citizens are *incensed rather than intimidated* by the Taliban losses in Afghanistan. Apart from sparse and isolated exceptions, our success in Afghanistan is not accomplishing a psychological victory among the terrorists and their tens of millions of supporters.

Over 70,000 terrorists have been trained by al Qaeda, and many thousands of these angry and trained young men have taken up quiet residences in Europe and America. They have been taught to be very patient, and to wait with alertness for their opportunity to inflict maximum terror on Americans. The November 3 issue of the *Los Angeles Times* reported on a conference briefing by terrorism expert Jerrold Post: "Post said he had interviewed suspected fundamentalist attackers and told the conference the results were 'startling and chilling.' Post said that when asked if there were any limits to the numbers of casualties they wanted to inflict, one suspect said: 'The more casualties, the better. The greater the number of casualties, the greater the measure of success.'"

In a videotaped statement in October, bin Laden himself affirmed the necrophilic obsession of the terrorists: "Yes, we kill their innocents." Ms. Julie Sirrs reported: "One Yemeni prisoner told me he would be willing to get on a school bus and kill children if the religious scholars told him to."

The November 7 issue of the *Los Angeles Times*

reported: "Asserting that Al Qaeda cells operate in more than 60 nations, Bush said that 'they are seeking chemical, biological and nuclear weapons.'" Bob Woodward, in the October 29 issue of the *Washington Post Weekly,* quoted a senior Bush administration official as conceding: "I don't think there has been such risk to the country since the Cuban missile crisis." That same issue of the *Washington Post Weekly* featured an informative article on the results of an Italian terrorist investigation involving, primarily, a 33-year-old Tunisian named Khemais:

> When Khemais moved to Milan [in March of 1998], the sources say, the structure of terrorist networks in Europe was changing. A group of violent, radical militants had left behind conflicts in Egypt and Algeria, and wars in Afghanistan, Bosnia and Chechnya, all of which were over or in abeyance. The "brothers," as the militants called themselves, soon found a new organizing principle in bin Laden's campaign against targets in the West, according to Italian investigators.
>
> The Algerian situation, for years the epicenter, has in the past few years lost its centrality in favor of a new binding capability represented by the project of bin Laden [that is, Islamic terrorist organizations worldwide have shifted their focus from the situations in their own countries to the bin Laden-sparked campaign against Americans], according to an April report by the Digos, the Italian anti-terrorism police. . .
>
> In March, bugs in Khemais's apartment picked up a conversation between the Tunisian and Lased Ben Heni, a 31-year-old Libyan veteran of the Afghan camps. "God loves us because Europe is in our hands . . . we are fighting-immigrants.

> This is our duty that we have to carry on with
> honor. . . We have to be like snakes. We have to
> strike and then hide."
> Khemais said in the bugged conversation,
> "Al Qaeda exists from Algeria to the
> Philippines. They're everywhere." . . . Most of
> those in the Frankfurt and Milan cells, including
> Khemais . . . are now in custody, but the Italian
> documents make clear that the European terrorist
> ranks are easily replenished with recruits.

The pattern of the terrorists is to strike and melt away. Lay low and let the target population drift toward a state of relief. When the target has allowed itself to become distracted, the calm is shattered by an unexpected strike of even higher magnitude. These are religiously inspired warriors whose minds are sold out unreservedly to murder and mayhem. Jim Hoagland wrote in the *Washington Post Weekly* about the time he spent observing Abu Nidal (the notorious terrorist mastermind who was given refuge by Saddam Hussein in the previous decade): "For Abu Nidal, killing was part and parcel of his identity. He would not exist without political murders to commit. The politics, in fact, counted little for him; murder was all."

The terrorist mass movement is properly understood as a global and sophisticated exercise in religious necrophilia. Their love of death has the core characteristics of a sexual-type obsession. They have consistently exhibited a monomaniacal and erotic-type passion for the sight of mangled corpses.

The state of madness that the terrorists and their supporters have reached is such that nothing short of a sudden and shocking encounter with superpower reality will prepare their minds for a civilized negotiation on the issues. If we think to show them goodwill (before first inducing a more sober state of mind among them), they will perceive this either as weakness or conspiratorial pretense. If we think to facilitate among them a more educated understanding of American values and policies, they will reject this out of hand. If we pressure their governments to allow free elections, the fundamentalist parties will sweep the room clean in countries from Algeria to Yemen. No fundamental improvements will be brought to the situation until we first implement the measure that the situation requires.

We can continue winning on the battlefields, but this "patient accumulation of successes" (the financial, military, diplomatic, etc.) will not address the problem at its generative level. We are slapping hard at the skin, but the imperative is to scrape out the marrow.

So long as we delay, the militants will enjoy the advantage of time. With each passing day the likelihood increases that the terrorists will secure devices of destruction that can hurt us in ways we do not like to think about.

8.   The Main Thesis

The militants place little value on their lives, yet there is something they value above their lives. We should not restrain ourselves from seizing the psychological advantage afforded by the vulnerability of what is most dear to them.

In the middle of the last century, millions of Germans wished to have no share in the campaign of the Nazis. They did not subscribe to the vision of Hitler, and they were appalled by the Nazi effort to exterminate the Jewish race. Yet these millions of civilized German people, although profoundly unsympathetic to the program of the Nazis, were unable or unwilling to halt the escalating madness of their compatriots. It therefore became the moral obligation of the civilized nations, and also their existential necessity, to destroy the German nation. This horrific destruction of Germany was a painful injustice to the millions of Germans who detested the Nazis. Yet the responsibility for this injustice cannot rightly be charged to the Allied nations, but rather to the Nazis. Since the civilized German people could not control the uncivilized German Nazis, our only reasonable option was to reduce the cities of Germany to rubble. Afterwards, when Germany was terrified into submission, and when the tens of millions of Nazi sympathizers had experienced a fundamental change of heart, we successfully helped Germany to rebuild and to reintegrate peacefully into the international economic and political system. Germany, which had pledged itself to the extermination of every non-Aryan element on the face of the earth, became one of the most peaceful nations in the history of the world. Germany also became an enduring friend and ally of the United States of America.

Although the campaign of the Islamic militants confronts us with a situation far more complicated, a definitive solution to the problem will require an audacity of logic in generic parallel with that which proved effective in ending World War II. There are millions of Muslims who do not subscribe to the vision of the militants, yet they have shown themselves unable or unwilling to halt the escalating madness of their co-religionists. Samuel P. Huntington was attempting to call our attention to this over five years ago: "If Muslims allege that the West wars on Islam and if Westerners allege that Islamic groups war on the West, it seems reasonable to conclude that something very much like a war is underway. . . American leaders allege that the Muslims involved in the quasi war are a small minority whose use of violence is rejected by the great majority of moderate Muslims. This may be true, but evidence to support it is lacking. Protests against anti-Western violence have been totally absent in Muslim countries. Muslim governments, even the bunker governments friendly to and dependent on the West, have been strikingly reticent when it comes to condemning terrorist acts against the West" (*The Clash of Civilizations and the Remaking of the World Order,* Simon & Schuster, 1996, p. 217).

Since September 11, we have valiantly accomplished little more than a cosmetic damage to our enemy. Our success in truly eliminating the Islamic terrorist threat will require a strategy well beyond the magnitude of what we are currently prosecuting. The strategy I am advancing would present an enormous injustice to the millions of Muslims who do not support the campaign of the militants, yet the responsibility for this injustice could not rightly be charged against the United States. The responsibility for the injustice would belong entirely to the terrorists and their tens of millions of supporters.

An implementation of this strategy would not make us feel good. To even discuss it is a disturbing experience. Yet on the other hand, how can we feel good at the thought of allowing this problem to continue for the next fifty years? Our lifetimes and the lifetimes of our children would be punctuated by horrific terrorist assaults and our nightly news programs dominated by a decades-long continuum of blood, guts, and fear. An upgraded strategy would not make us feel good, but it would promise to accomplish our immediate objectives, and afterward we could heartily assist these shell-shocked societies in developing and integrating, peacefully and successfully, into the international system. Until we seize the initiative, and assume the necessary audacity, there is no possibility of hope for children such as the trembling and weeping Palestinian boys and girls whose pictures we routinely see in our daily newspapers. Today their tender souls yearn for safety, warmth, and kindness. But if we fail in our obligation to bring this terror to a swift and decisive end, these lovely and delicate children are likely to become tomorrow's suicide bombers.

Osama bin Laden stated in 1998: "For Muslims, no piece of land . . . compares in significance with Arabia and Iraq" (quoted by Jim Hoagland in the October 1 issue of the *Washington Post Weekly*). Baghdad was the capital of the vast and powerful Abbasid caliphate, dominating the Middle East from the eighth century until the middle of the thirteenth. Since the theocratic vision of the Islamic militants involves the reconstitution of a centralized Islamic empire, first encompassing the Middle East and eventually the entire world, Iraq is sacred as the historical symbol of the vision pursued by the terrorists.

When the army of Saddam Hussein invaded Kuwait in the summer of 1990, thereby occupying the principal buffer between Iraq and the oil fields of Arabia, the Saudi ruling family accepted the offer of the U.S. to intervene militarily. America built advanced bases and established a direct military presence on Saudi Arabian soil. To bin Laden, and to many other Muslims throughout the world, this was an act of extreme sacrilege. Not only would a non-Islamic people be warring against Islamic Iraq, but "infidel" troops would be stationed in Arabia, which hosts the two holiest sites of Islam (Mecca and Medina), and which does not permit non-Muslims to be buried in its soil. The presence of American troops in Arabia, and the Western bombing of Iraq, are two of the principal grievances of the Islamic fundamentalists. The crucial point is the value given to Iraq and Arabia by the terrorists, and most emphatically the value given to the Arabian holy places of Mecca and Medina.

The terrorists have threatened us with nuclear weapons, and have boasted of destroying our landmarks. The government-sponsored Egyptian newspaper, *Al Akhbar,* has openly called for the destruction of the Statue of Liberty. (To my knowledge, no one in the Arab world, and particularly no one in the Egyptian government that controls *Al Akhbar,* has condemned or even criticized this article. The article also praised Adolph Hitler as a saint and complained that he had not "finished the job" (see *The New Yorker,* October 8, article by Jeffrey Goldberg)). It is no longer a secret that our own government has known of the terrorists' pursuit of nuclear and biological weapons for close to a decade. Although it seems unlikely that the terrorists have obtained nuclear weapons, it is generally acknowledged that the threat to America of a nuclear or a biological attack is looming larger with time, in spite of our multi-dimensional successes since early October.

The December 7 issue of the *Los Angeles Times* reported the following from Russia: "Russian police have arrested seven people accused of trying to sell more than two pounds of highly enriched weapons-grade uranium, Russian television said. The men, arrested . . . just east of Moscow, were trying to sell a capsule containing uranium–235 for $30,000, NTV television said."

For each plot foiled, how many have succeeded? To quote again from Representative Christopher Shays: "I'm *absolutely convinced* we'll have a chemical, biological, or nuclear attack. The question is not *if,* it's when, where, and what the magnitude will be" (emphasis mine).

Shay is a ranking member of the U.S. House of Representatives, not a partially informed fanatic. Military historian John Keegan observed: "Western intelligence agencies believe that no terrorist organization has yet acquired a nuclear capability. But they also know it will be only a matter of time before one does, unless stringent measures are taken."

A nuclear or a biological attack on American soil could threaten an upheaval in our way of life for many years to come. We could not possibly calculate the devastating social, economic, political, and psychological effect this would have on the future of our country. Whereas the attacks of September 11 unified us in emotion and in purpose, and galvanized our support for the political leadership of the country, a successful *nuclear strike* in America could threaten to rip us apart with disbelief and terror. A successful nuclear strike within America could threaten to destroy all meaningful confidence in the government of the United States. With these things in mind, it is safe to assert that no reasonably formulated *deterrent* to such a potential attack can be considered "too radical." My proposal for an immediate, viable, and effective deterrent can be stated quite simply: A nuclear, chemical, or biological attack by Islamic terrorists against America would forfeit the existence of what is most sacred to the Islamic terrorists.

While this could seem radically *unjust* to the many millions of civilized Muslims who do not support the terrorists, the *injustice* would be on the part of the terrorists rather than on the government of the United States. If a formal, public warning were issued, to the effect that such an attack by Islamic terrorists would cancel the existence of the spiritual landmarks most sacred to the terrorists, then any conceivable scenario along these lines would consign the provocating factor—and therefore *the full responsibility*—to the Islamic terrorists and those who have supported them.

No country on earth is more directly responsible for financially supporting both the development and the destructive capacity of the Islamic terrorist movement than our pseudo-friend, Saudi Arabia.

It is increasingly clear that the bin Laden brand of religious extremism was incubated in the Saudi heartlands. . . Anti-American sentiment is now shared not only by religious extremists, but by ordinary Saudis." (*The Economist,* October 28)

[Political leaders have been insisting] that those sympathetic with the terrorists are a "tiny minority" of Muslims, and that the vast majority is appalled by what happened. It is important for them to say this to prevent Muslims as a group from becoming targets of hatred. The problem is that dislike and hatred of America and what it stands for are clearly much more widespread than that. . . By this standard, sympathy for the terrorists is characteristic of much more than a "tiny minority" of Muslims." (Francis Fukuyama, writing in the October 5 issue of the *Wall Street Journal*)

Saudi Arabia . . . [is] by far the more repressive, secretive, and undemocratic of the two [contrasting with *Iran*]. . . And the stern form of Islam that dominates Saudi Arabia is not a million miles from the Taliban's own religious practices.

To cap it all, the Saudi authorities have been reluctant to give the FBI the assistance it needs to trace the contacts and background of the hijackers. . . It is recollected that the [Saudi] authorities were equally uncooperative after 19 American servicemen were killed by a bomb explosion at their Al Khobar barracks in Saudi Arabia in 1996. . .

The repressiveness of its laws, its total absence of democracy, its opaqueness, the corruption and venality of some of its myriad princes, are suddenly seen anew. . . There is a sniff of double standards in the air [a reference to Western policies toward Iran and Saudi Arabia]: the support that Iran gives to Palestinian [terrorist] groups, such as Hamas, is probably less than these groups are getting from Saudi Arabia. (*The Economist,* November 10)

Not only the financial provisions that have fueled the capacity of the terrorist movement, but also a principal source of terrorist manpower has been provided by the country of Saudi Arabia:

Saudi Arabia . . . provided 15 of the 19 hijackers and refuses to freeze terrorist assets. (*The Economist,* October 13)

The Saudi regime has played a dangerous game. It deflects attention from its shoddy record at home by funding religious schools (madrasas) and centers that spread a rigid, puritanical brand of Islam—Wahhabism. In the past 30 years

Saudi-funded schools have churned out tens of thousands of half-educated, fanatical Muslims who view the modern world and non-Muslims with great suspicion. America in this world view is almost always evil. (Fareed Zakaria, *Newsweek,* October 15)

Retired Army Lieutenant Colonel Ralph Peters wrote for the September 14 issue of the *Wall Street Journal,* with regard to the poisonous religious schools (madrasas) funded worldwide by Saudi Arabian money: "[The madrasas] that are being used specifically to raise terrorists . . . are legitimate targets and should be attacked, promptly and thoroughly."

Saudi Arabian money has been the principal source of funding for the now-extinct terrorist training camps in Afghanistan and Sudan, which have flooded the world with thousands of trained and indoctrinated aspiring mass murderers, and Saudi money has been the chief source of funding for high-level terrorist operations worldwide. Although wealthy Saudis have expanded into various industries and spheres of entrepreneurship, the flourishing business climate there was created almost exclusively by the enormous revenues accruing from Saudi oil. The annihilation of the World Trade Center and of the bodies immolated within it was purchased, primarily and ultimately, with Saudi Arabian oil revenues. One of the most perversely audacious public acts since September 11 was the chiding lecture a Saudi prince attempted to impose on the mayor of New York City in the course of handing the mayor a Judas check for $10 million (the mayor responded with immaculate integrity). We would have preferred from the prince an apology for the Saudi money that financed the destruction, and for the Saudi manpower that accomplished it, and we would have preferred prompt and straightforward cooperation in the early stages of the investigation. We are not wanting for money to rebuild, but we are wanting for the presence of family members and friends who can never be replaced. But the Saudi royal family and the terrorist community it has cultivated do not relate to life on such terms.

We should seize the advantage of the terms on which they do relate, rather than holding our foreign policy hostage to Saudi contracts with major American oil corporations. There are other ways of obtaining the oil we need.

Since Saudi oil money was the watershed source of funding for what led to the slaughter of Americans in New York City, Virginia, and Pennsylvania, we should therefore consider the legitimacy of the inverse purchase of U.S. prerogative by the blood and ashes of these thousands of Americans. This U.S. prerogative, purchased with the blood of our men, women, and children, extends with absolute justification to the oil fields of Saudi Arabia, just as it extends to other spheres of real estate should the Saudi-financed terrorist movement ever again assault America as it did on September 11. (Our government may or may not choose to exercise this prerogative. Yet no one can legitimately deny the prerogative itself.)

In 1973, to afflict us for our support of Israel in defending itself successfully against the surprise genocidal war-campaign of Syria, Egypt, and Iraq, the Saudi-led OPEC withheld its oil from the United States. This action plunged our country into a ten-year recession that disrupted business and credit patterns and led to the loss of jobs and homes for tens of thousands of hard-working Americans. Since September 11, numerous members of OPEC have been issuing veiled threats of another such embargo should the U.S. pursue Islamic terrorists into an Arab country. We should consider our full range of options in the face of such a civilizational threat. Although Russia, Canada, Mexico, and others could provide sufficient oil to keep us temporarily afloat, such an embargo would threaten to escalate numerous negative trends in the world situation. An OPEC oil embargo should never again be tolerated by Western governments. Our ability to act commensurately in 1973 was restricted by the formidable realities of the Cold War. No such realities exist today.

The functioning of Western nations has grown so dependent on oil that a threat to our supply is *the qualitative equivalent* of a declaration of war. In this our prerogative has been doubly reinforced.

Early in the seventh century, the Islamic Arab armies swept out of the Peninsula and stormed the surrounding nations. Within less than a century, the land grab had extended through Persia in the east, Asia Minor in the north, and Egypt, North Africa, and Spain in the west. Although a considerable portion of this land, as with Persia and Spain, was retaken over the centuries, and Asia Minor now belongs to the Turks, many other countries and regions, such as Egypt, Syria, and Mesopotamia (now Iraq), have remained in the possession of the Arabs. Prior to the seventh century, these lands had belonged to other peoples. The Islamic Arabs took these foreign lands by force, in a brutal series of unprovoked wars and massacres, and made them their own. For all of their allegations against "American and Jewish imperialism," it has never bothered the Arabs that all of the "Arab nations" outside the Arabian peninsula were acquired by means of brutally imperialistic takeovers. I am hardly suggesting they have no legitimate claim to these lands. My point is that the legitimacy of their claim rests on the power of the sword, including their claim to *Palestine.*

If some of this land were taken back from them by the power of "the sword," how could such a thing be construed as *illegitimate*? Only our most distorted public pieties could levy upon our logic the disadvantage of conceding the prerogative of power to the terrorist-supporting Arab states, while forfeiting that prerogative for ourselves.

America is democracy, and America owes nothing to governments that repress freedom—absolutely nothing. The Saudi Arabian government is a more repressive and brutal regime than that of the Chinese communists or of Fidel Castro's Cuba. The Saudi rulers know everything said and done in the mosques and in the banks of their kingdom. Saudi Arabian wealth has fused with Saudi Arabian religious fanaticism to breed a global network of well-funded and highly motivated Islamic mass murderers. Saudi oil and Saudi fanaticism are the *root sources* of the violence that led to the mass immolation of Americans on September 11.

In terms of realpolitik, Saudi Arabia's only legitimate claim to its real estate is whatever force it can muster to defend what it occupies. The earth belongs to those who occupy, and occupation is contingent on the success of power. In rejecting the modern world, the Arab nations have lost the contest of power.

Yet they have cultivated a psychology of denial, and they will not desist from their program of terror until this psychology has been destroyed. I do not believe our daisy cutters, Special Forces, financial roadblocks, and diplomatic pressures will ever accomplish this correction of twisted logic in the minds of our enemies. We can slow things down by these methods, but we will not root them out. The madness of our enemies is out of control, with no hope for a solution by means of a "patient accumulation of successes." The only measure capable of bringing their violent illness into remission is shock.

I am advancing a formula that would address the Islamic terrorist threat at its generative source. This formula advises the U.S. government to issue a public assurance that if America is ever again assaulted by terrorists, we will eliminate the most valued landmarks of the terrorists, and we will confiscate the most valuable oil fields of

Saudi Arabia and Iraq.

To the militants, Mecca is a spiritual landmark testifying that Allah has claimed the earth as the rightful province of fundamentalist Islam, and that Allah will bless their efforts to destroy every non-Islamic society in the world. They interpret the current situation as a *religious war* between non-Islamic societies and the warriors of Allah. Until we confront them at this level, we have no realistic chance of truly defeating them. Until we dismantle their psychology at its source, nothing we do will threaten the religiously inspired confidence that their god will bless their efforts to destroy America and every other non-Islamic society.

The militants have attacked our landmarks and boasted of more to come. They have called for the destruction of the Statue of Liberty and of the civilization it symbolizes. They are the enemies of freedom, of humanity, and of any justifiable concept of God. We should make them deeply aware that *their* landmarks are far more vulnerable to our weapons than our landmarks are to their weapons. Such a measure would be deeply painful to many who do not subscribe to the vision of the militants, but their unwillingness or inability to dismantle the militants' vision leaves *us* with the responsibility of doing precisely that. The injustice of such a measure could not legitimately be charged against the government of the United States. The responsibility lies entirely with the terrorists and with their tens of millions of supporters. The prosecution of this strategy would not make us feel good, but we have no apologies to offer.

Our enemies assume we will remain hamstrung by our ideology, and that our public pieties will restrain us from a commensurate response to the threat they have mounted against us. So long as we allow them to believe this, we will not have won the psychological war. Therefore, in spite of all of our battlefield victories and our "patient accumulation of successes," we will leave the conclusion of this war to future generations who will despise us for failing to answer the uncomfortable requirements of our time.

I will close this eighth article by once again quoting the defining insight as expounded by former Senator Sam Nunn: "Until this psychological war is waged effectively, we will eliminate 10 terrorist cells but do it in a way that creates 20 new ones; that is not progress. . . This psychological war is the key to whether our children and grandchildren will be plagued years from now."

9.   Principled Compassion

We will not effectively address the inner source of the Islamic terrorist threat until we boldly confront its concept of God. This could be swiftly accomplished by the introduction of our ultimate capacity in connection with the spiritual landmarks of the militants.

Five times a day, every day, the militants bow with their faces to the ground and their heads pointed in the direction of Mecca. Their concept of God is inextricably bound up with this place that they look upon with sacred awe. It is the earthly headquarters of their god, and every Muslim is commanded to journey to Mecca, if at all possible, at least once in his or her lifetime.

The terrorists' destruction of our landmarks on September 11 was interpreted by them as a spiritual signal that American civilization would now begin to collapse at the hands of warriors under the blessing of Allah. Until this belief is destroyed in their minds, the terrorist mass movement will not lose its inner momentum, and the militants will not desist from their commitment to the slaughter of Americans. The militants interpret the current situation as a holy war between Allah and the West. We must now bring this war to a showdown, and thereby determine for them the stronger party.

The threat of using conventional weapons against the spiritual landmarks of the terrorists would likely provoke resistance rather than trembling, since conventional weapons generally produce a destruction that can be repaired. Such an assault on their landmarks would likely be construed as a challenge rather than a defeat. In contrast, we have weapons that would render the region of their landmarks unrecognizable and uninhabitable.

The holy book of the terrorists commands them to journey at least once in their lifetimes to the earthly headquarters of their god, and to pray five times each day with their faces pointed in the direction of that sacred landmark. How could their religiously inspired confidence against America be sustained if their most sacred landmark were transformed into a spectacular testimony of the military power of the United States? The militants are currently viewed by tens of millions of Muslims as the heroes of Islam, but we have the capacity to create events that would show them to be the destroyers of Islam.

When America saw pictures of the aftermath in Hiroshima, there was no joy or satisfaction in our collective soul. Stating this in terms of the logic recently summarized by Thomas L. Friedman: We had not done something that made us feel good, but we *had* done something that made our enemies feel very bad. In doing this, we had crushed their myth, and thereby brought the war to a screeching halt. Not only were many lives and much suffering spared in the broader calculation, but also an evil vision was destroyed and an entire civilization brought back to its senses.

Today it is within our power to execute a set of military decisions that would promise to halt the terrorists' march of destruction. This measure would not make us feel good, but it would emasculate the myth that informs and fuels the generative activity of the international terrorist movement. We have a definitive historical precedent, and we ought to study it very carefully. A nuclear-enforced world order is not the best of all possible worlds, but it may be the only means of avoiding the worst of all possible worlds. The thought is disturbing, but perhaps the time has come. (Haven't we always known it would arrive eventually?)

Thomas Friedman recently wrote: "Every state has to know that after Sept. 11, harboring anti-U.S. terrorists will be lethal. To drive that point home, though, people have to see that we are focused, serious and ready to use whatever tactics will make the terrorists feel bad, not make us feel good" (quoted from the *Vacaville Reporter*).

I am not suggesting Mr. Friedman had nuclear weapons in mind when he wrote this. But the force of his logic leads naturally to the question of why the "use of whatever tactics" should preclude the use of the ultimate and most decisive tactic? Particularly in view of the mounting evidence that no other tactic can realistically promise to accomplish either our immediate or our long-term objectives?

We have allowed our nuclear capabilities to become virtually irrelevant in the realpolitik of world affairs. Governments, nations, and parties have simply ceased to feel intimidated by the potential of our ultimate weapons, and this is so because they believe our ideology will prevent us from ever using these weapons against them.

An article by Dana Milbank in the October 15 issue of the *Post Weekly Edition* reported the following:

> The Sept. 11 terrorist attacks on Washington and New York have invigorated national security strategists inside and outside the government who favor using nuclear arms to deter and respond to chemical or biological attacks. . . Many Bush administration officials have endorsed the notion of switching to smaller nuclear arms that could be used for, among other things, hitting chemical and biological weapons sites. . . The chairman of the Joint Chiefs of Staff, Gen. Richard G. Meyers, during his confirmation hearing Sept. 13 . . . pointed out that the military already has "a number of low-yield weapons in the current stockpile." . . . Southwest Missouri State University's William R. Van Cleave . . . whose colleague [at the National Institute for Public Policy], J. D. Crouch, is now assistant under-secretary of Defense for international security policy, says

some Bush advisors "believe *we have marginal-
ized nuclear weapons too much. We have removed
them from extended deterrence too much.*"
(Emphasis mine)

The strategy I am advancing at this point could not
succeed as a stand-alone measure, and the formula proposed
in this book will be more fully developed in the following
articles. But the principal thrust of my argument involves a
straightforward and inviolable connection between asymmetrical terrorist warfare, the U.S. nuclear arsenal, and the
most sacred landmarks of the militants.

Those who support or sympathize with this threat to
our country must be made to understand that they are placing themselves in a jeopardy beyond anything they have ever
previously imagined.

The use of our ultimate strength, in connection with
the most sacred places of the enemy, would be a painful sacrifice in the name of compassion and the vision of a safer
world. It would give us no pleasure, and we would feel no
pride, but it would promise to accomplish our objectives and
restore the security we desire for our children.

Early in World War II, the British had cracked the
German code and were obtaining critical information about
the formation, strategies, and broad objectives of the Nazi
regime. In November 1940, the British leadership was suddenly faced with an excruciating dilemma. It was learned that
the German Luftwaffe (air force) would be sending a
squadron of bombers in a surprise attack on the English city
of Coventry. To mount a defense against the "surprise" attack
would have served notice to the Germans that their code had
been deciphered. At this critical early stage in the war, the
British government under Winston Churchill decided that
their deep access to German intelligence was indispensable
to the overall war effort. The city of Coventry was sacrificed.

Over five hundred houses were destroyed in the center of the city, along with many inhabitants of those houses.

Churchill was no beast. In that war with the Nazis, civilization itself was hanging in the balance. It is difficult to imagine a more agonizing dilemma, but Churchill understood what was at stake and he boldly sacrificed a city for the broader advantage of mankind. Churchill stared the Devil in the eye and refused to blink. Had he wilted under the pressure, and restricted his logic to a smaller set of moral principles, he would have compromised the security of England on a much greater scale. Yet it was not only England that the Nazis were aiming to destroy, but also the very concept of civilization. After the demise of the Third Reich in 1945, nothing so heinous has threatened the world until the present hour. Not even the horrors of international communism presented such a macabre threat as that posed by the Nazis sixty years ago or the terrorist mass movement of today. Al Qaeda, in the broadest sense of what that term represents, must be eliminated at all costs. Bin Laden himself warned us: "I swear to God that America will not live in peace." And al-Qaeda's spokesman warned us: "The Americans must know that the storm of airplanes will not stop."

Faced with a similar evil in his own era, Winston Churchill gave a city to destruction in the name of a more far-reaching moral conviction. He understood that for *every day* in which the Nazi regime was able to continue in existence, death and destruction would accumulate throughout the world. In an act of principled compassion and definitive regard for the welfare of mankind, the British leadership yielded up Coventry as a tragic and redeeming sacrifice.

If our own situation were to require something similar (although involving a foreign coordinate), do we have the will for such a thing? If not, I suggest we have no hope of defeating what currently threatens us. We can slow it down, hinder it, and bruise it. But the spiritual resolve of the militants will not die, and the terrorist movement will continue self-repli-cating, until we destroy it in the spirit of its mind.

There are situations in which an accepted framework of moral logic, effective and praiseworthy within its appropriate context of application, actually becomes *immoral* if it is allowed to compromise a vastly greater ethical imperative. The Bible itself, in both the Old and New Testaments, repeatedly attests to such a complexity of moral reality.

The biblical doctrine of war is not inconsistent with the other teachings of the Old and New Testaments. According to the Bible, the supremely violent event in the human drama is the second coming of Jesus Christ (all Bible quotations are from the New King James version, Thomas Nelson Publishers, 1982):

> When the Lord Jesus is revealed from heaven with His mighty angels, in flaming fire taking vengeance on those who do not know God, and on those who do not obey the gospel of our Lord Jesus Christ. These shall be punished with everlasting destruction from the presence of the Lord and from the glory of His power. (2 Thessalonians 1:7–9)

> Therefore as the tares are gathered and burned in the fire, so it will be at the end of this age. The Son of Man will send out His angels, and they will gather out of His kingdom all things that offend, and those who practice lawlessness, and will cast them into the furnace of fire. There will be wailing and gnashing of teeth. (Matthew 13:40–42)

Jesus is the one who instructed His disciples to "turn the other cheek," and who set the example Himself:

I gave My back to those who struck Me,
And My cheeks to those who plucked out the
beard; I did not hide My face from shame and
spitting. (Isaiah 50:6)

Then they spat in His face and beat Him; and
others struck Him with the palms of their hands.
(Matthew 26:67)

Who, when He was reviled, did not revile in
return; when He suffered, He did not threaten. (1
Peter 2:23)

You have heard that it was said, "An eye for
an eye and a tooth for a tooth." But I tell you not
to resist an evil person. But whoever slaps you on
your right cheek, turn the other to him also.
(Matthew 5:38, 39)

Yet the Bible says in another place:

Therefore whoever resists the authority
resists the ordinance of God, and those who resist
will bring judgment on themselves. For rulers are
not a terror to good works, but to evil. Do you
want to be unafraid of the authority? Do what is
good, and you will have praise from the same.
For he is God's minister to you for good. But if
you do evil, be afraid; for he does not bear the
sword in vain; for he is God's minister, an
avenger to execute wrath on him who practices
evil. (Romans 13:2–4)

According to this passage, the Bible authorizes and
requires the state to function as "an avenger to execute wrath

on him who practices evil. . . For rulers are not a terror to good works, but to evil." The Bible attests in another place:

> Therefore submit yourselves to every ordinance of man [meaning "the law of the land"] for the Lord's sake, whether to the king as supreme, or to governors, as to those who are sent by him [the government] for the punishment of evildoers and for the praise of those who do good. (1 Peter 2:13, 14)

In one context, a Christian is instructed "not to resist an evil person." In another context, the same Christian is instructed to "execute wrath on him who practices evil."

The Bible cannot legitimately be used to call into question the current ethical imperative that history has thrust into the hands of the Unites States government. This imperative is the rapid and comprehensive elimination of the anti-civilization symbolized in the Taliban/al Qaeda.

If the fulfillment of our moral obligation, and the prosecution of our most immediate existential imperative, were to involve the use of nuclear weapons in connection with the holy places of the Islamic warriors, then our regard for the broader advantage of mankind will compel us to do what we must.

Such a decision would not lead us in the direction of barbarism, but rather away from it. Ralph Peters wrote for the October 1 issue of *The Washington Post Weekly:* "[There are many who argue that] if we adopt ferocious means of fighting back against our enemies, we will become just like them. This is nonsense. In World War II, we responded to Japanese and German savagery with indescribable brutality of our own. We firebombed the cities of our enemies and ended the war by dropping atomic bombs. On the bitterly contested islands of the Pacific, our GIs did not read Japanese soldiers their rights before burning them to death with flamethrowers. Yet the men and women of the 'Greatest Generation' did not come home to stage a military coup. They came back, gladly, to peace, liberal democracy, and the GI Bill. We must recognize that this is a new age, with new rules and new requirements."

Today we are confronted with an enemy that has linked its perverse concept of God to its war of terror against America. Although we can cause our enemies to stumble under our current measures, we will not defeat them until we transform the vision they carry in the spirit of their mind.

When we compelled Hirohito to relinquish his claims to Deity, only then had we truly won the war against the militant Japanese. The measures we took in the summer of 1945 brought the warrior leadership of Japan to its knees. A parallel measure will be required for a genuine defeat of the Islamic terrorist movement.

Our introduction of nuclear weapons in 1945 did not usher in an area of barbarism for America. On the contrary, we picked up the pieces after World War II and launched the most extraordinary era of social, economic, and political growth that any nation has ever witnessed at any time in recorded history.

Postscript to Article Nine

"I see water and buildings. O my God! O my God!"

We cannot forget the holocaust accomplished by Islamic militants in New York City, Pennsylvania, and Virginia, the spectacular exhibition of depravity witnessed by every one of us. We cannot—we must not—let our memory ever grow dull. What we have seen with our eyes and felt in our souls must now guide us in deciding what needs to be done. How many priceless dreams were smashed and vaporized, and life-long efforts mocked in the slaughter? And in the days since then, the enemy taunts us from his hiding places: "There is America, hit by God in one of its softest spots. Thank God for that." "The Americans must know that the storm of airplanes will not stop."

How long do we live with dread and anxiety over what the next news report will be, when it is within our power to swiftly bring down this threat?

A condition of prolonged anxiety invites dangerous consequences to the health of an individual as well as to a collective psyche. A carefully measured investment of our ultimate capacity would not lead us toward the path of psychic disintegration, but it may be the only measure that can keep us from that path.

We have 103 nuclear power plants vulnerable to small aircraft packed with explosives (why no anti-aircraft installations?). We have a food chain with millions of blind spots. We have scores of chemical plants, and thousands of dams, reservoirs, and busy bridges. There is no end to the possibilities of a massive viral, bacterial, or chemical assault. Our land stretches out for thousands of miles, free and beautiful land! Our interests are spread across the earth. How will adequate protection on such a scale ever be provided? Only by an offensive of overwhelming effect.

For every loss resulting from such a measure, there would be incalculable sparing of life and property in the broader calculation. There is no foreseeable end to the death and destruction that will accumulate within the parameters of the present order if it is allowed to continue.

The painful toll extracted by such an offensive would be a tragic yet redeeming purchase price for the demise of an anti-civilization that has the commitment and the potential of bringing slaughter to the homes of millions, and corrosion to the dreams of America itself. Protection and a return to security will never be purchased apart from a willingness to do what we are capable of doing. If we wait too long, even our final option will be fatally compromised.

10.   The Role of the Russians

An assurance to the world that we are prepared to introduce our ultimate weapons, in connection with the sites most sacred to the enemy, would be of questionable wisdom without the consent of Russia. Yet the Russians would have compelling reasons for consent if they were made equal participants in such a peacemaking mission.

The Russian people were Christianized over one thousand years ago, about three hundred years after the Christianization of England, and eight hundred years before the founding of the United States. For much of the twentieth century, the idea of "Russia" was equated with "Soviet Union" and "atheistic communism." Although there were good reasons for this, to be "Russian" is something far more profound and enduring than any of the varying politico-economic systems that have characterized the eras of Russian history. To be a Russian is to be, among other things, a Euro-Slavic person from a nation whose religion, by general consensus, is Christian. *The Economist* reported in its October 6 issue: "Last week [Russian President Vladimir Putin] pulled off a hugely successful coup in Germany, where he wowed parliament with a speech delivered in fluent German and dotted with erudite references to Kant and Schiller. Russia, he said, was *rooted in European values*" (emphasis mine).

These common values alluded to by Mr. Putin trace back most emphatically to the fourth century, but also much earlier. The formal Christianization of the Roman Empire began in the year 312, when Constantine I took control of Rome after a battle in which he had ordered his army to sew insignias of a Christian cross underneath the standard eagle on their banners. From that time, the eagle and the cross became the crowning symbols of the civilization that had been launched from Rome. About twenty years later,

Constantine transferred the capital of the Empire to the Grecian city of Byzantium, renaming it *Constantinople* (now called Istanbul). After his death in 336, the Empire progressively split into western and eastern legs, obtaining its formal and definitive separation in the year 1054.

The Roman Empire, as a concept and an essence, did not end with "the fall of Rome" in the fifth century. In concept, essence, and aspiration, the Empire continued in a northwest direction through continental Europe, where Germanic rulers were successively crowned "Holy Roman Emperor" from the year 800 (beginning with Charlemagne) until the formal termination of the Holy Roman Empire in 1806 (by the decree of Napoleon). Even after this, the emperors of Germany were called *Kaisers* until the end of World War I. "Kaiser" is a Germanized form of the title "Caesar" (which the Romans pronounced with a hard "c").

In the east, Roman emperors continued to reign out of Constantinople until the Muslim conquest of that city in 1453, which ended the reign of the last Byzantine-Roman Emperor, Constantine XI. Constantine arranged for his niece, Sophia, to be given in marriage to Ivan III, the Grand Duke of Moscow. From that time, the Russian royalty believed itself the legitimate continuation of the Roman Empire. Ivan began calling himself *Czar,* a Russianized form of Caesar, and referred to Moscow as "the Third Rome" (Constantinople having been the second). Ivan also adopted as his state symbol the Holy Roman imperial emblem of a double-headed eagle under a single crown (representing the eastern and western divisions of the Empire and the dormant spiritual vision of an eventually reunited Empire). Sophia transformed the royal customs of Moscow into a modified replica of what she had known in Constantinople, and Italian architects were imported to build churches and palaces.

In 1547, Ivan IV (grandson of Ivan III) became the

first Grand Duke of Moscow to be officially crowned as
Czar. He marred Anastasia, whose powerful aristocratic
family had recently taken the name *Romanov.* In the year
1613, Anastasia's family gained control of the throne, initiating the dynasty of *Romanov Czars* that continued until the
execution of Nicholas II by the Bolsheviks in 1918.
(Nicholas' youngest daughter, also named Anastasia, was
immortalized in a 1967 song by the Rolling Stones, titled
"Sympathy for the Devil.")

With the rise of the Romanov Czars, as historian
Norman Davies observes: "The Russians had found their
dynasty, and their national identity" (*Europe,* Oxford
University Press, 1996, p. 558). The Russians, a profoundly
Christian people, were now ruled by the Christian Caesars
of the Third Rome.

At the beginning of the eighteenth century, Russian
civilization lurched westward under the leadership of Czar
Peter I ("the Great"). During that century, Russia emerged
as a dominant European power. In 1767, Empress Catherine
officially declared Russia "a European state." After the
defeat of Napoleon in 1815, Czar Alexander I joined with
Germany and Austria in "The Holy Alliance." This aimed to
promote throughout Europe a stricter Christian orientation
as a counter to the secularizing influences of the
Enlightenment, and most emphatically to counter the
spreading atheism that, quite naturally, repudiated the doctrine of "the Divine right of kings." The Romanovs married
heavily into the European royal families (it is said that the
royal family in England is blood related to the Romanov
Czars), and became an important fixture in the political and
social milieu of Europe.

Russia was a leading member of the "Concert of
Europe," a nineteenth-century pact of solidarity that
included Britain, France, Austria, and Germany. But this
increasing immersion in European culture was generating a

reaction among some of the leading Russian intellectuals. The nineteenth-century intellectual scene in Russia was in no small measure occupied with the debate between the pragmatic "Westernizers" and the more romantic, myth-infatuated "Slavophiles." The latter (as exemplified in the later novels of Dostoevsky) argued that Russian civilization found its meaning in the Russian Orthodox Church, the Czar, and an agriculture-based economy that naturally promoted tight-knit peasant communities (mirs) and the social stability that tends to go with this. The Westernizers, for their part, calmly recognized that European technology, and European experiments with more efficient forms of government, were threatening to leave Russia far behind.

When the Bolsheviks took control of Russia near the end of World War II, their dominant visionaries (Lenin and Trotsky) were cosmopolitans who believed the Bolshevik movement was firmly in the tradition of the French Revolution. Lenin decreed that Russia must industrialize, collectivize, and de-mythologize. Atheistic communism began its first major experiment. The Cross and the Eagle were replaced by the Hammer and the Sickle, and the seventy-year effort to impose a totalitarian communist model on the world of nations was launched.

There were many Slavophiles within the Bolshevik party, but they had little influence on the Russian communist vision until after Lenin's death in 1924, and Trotsky's expulsion from the party in 1927. Although Stalin did not a bandon the vision of a global takeover by the communists (Marx's system collapses if this article is removed), his more immediate concern was for the consolidation, defense, and internal strengthening of the gains already made. Under Stalin's dictatorial leadership, the Russian-dominated union of socialist republics strove (unsuccessfully) to cultivate among their people a paranoid suspicion of all things "Western." Among the Russian leaders themselves, the tension between Slavophilia and internationalism played out as a slow-moving seesaw.

The period of the Cold War, beginning immediately after World War II, saw the ebb and flow of the expansionist impulse, with the high point of détente (early 1970s) followed by the 1979 invasion of Afghanistan and the consequent escalation of tension with America. The Cold War reached one of its peaks in 1985, when President Ronald Reagan publicly branded the Soviet Union as "an evil empire." During the 1980s, the buildup of the U.S. military under Reagan combined with the simply unsustainable Soviet myth of economic strength to force a historic capitulation of the Soviet Union under Gorbachev. The Cold War was over, but now what?

Russia's seventy-year experiment with communism was a fascinating and transforming episode in world history, but the relevant point here is that the experiment was an aberration in Russian history. The communist experiment was not a genuine expression of Russian culture. The Russians are not a godless or freedom-hating people. They are fiercely proud of their Slavic identity, but the only thing they seem to hate about Europe is the atheistic politico-economic model imported from Europe by Russian intellectuals and revolutionaries in the nineteenth and early twentieth centuries. Although they did not, as a general rule, experience the Reformation or the Enlightenment, they do not feel threatened by either of these defining Euro-American experiences. They have no problem with our fundamental values.

Russia is no longer the head of a communistic-atheistic empire aiming for world domination and the destruction of democracy. It has an elected, secular government with a predominately Christian population edging toward the ideals of social pluralism and free-market economics. Its culture is such that its people do not feel threatened by a president (Putin) who is more "authoritarian" than our culture would allow for. Putin is a democrat, and we should not be so quick to view him otherwise when he responds to national crises in a fashion more consistent with historical Russian culture than with our own. (Neither ought we be so quick to question Israel's commitment to democracy when it formulates policies consistent with its own security and cultural imperatives, rather than according to what we in our luxury have promoted as the only true form of democracy.)

In Russia there will always be "Slavophiles" and "Westernizers," just as we will always have our "Isolationists" and "Globalists." But the Russians are a Christianized people at heart with a deep and enduring love for freedom and progress. The Slavic pride is by no means an obstacle to a civilizational rapprochement with the United States and Europe, and perhaps the deliberately high-profile friendship of Presidents Bush and Putin is aimed at fostering a broad consensus in favor of such a development.

There are many compelling reasons for the pursuit of a comprehensive alliance of Russia, Europe, and the United States. Chief among these reasons is the current threat of the anti-civilization of Islamic fundamentalism. Samuel P. Huntington observes: "States respond primarily to perceived threats" (*Clash of Civilizations*, op. cit., p. 34).

It was a perceived threat that compelled America and western Europe to form, along with Turkey, the North Atlantic Treaty Organization in 1949. The threat at that time was the violent advance of international communism. NATO was formed in reaction to the threat of the Russian-dominated Soviet Union and its satellite states. Today, that particular threat exists only in the paranoia of some of our old-school Cold War warriors. The very nation that NATO was formed to counter has passed through its episode of experimentation with an ideology that was foreign even to its own culture. Now that the shameful episode has run its course, we should consider that Russia's more natural place is *within* NATO.

Over a month before the summit, Putin was already sounding out bold ideas among the U.S. and European leadership. Jim Hoaglund wrote in the October 15 issue of the *Post Weekly:* "In Brussels on Oct. 3, Putin made a skillful bid to enlarge the opening for Russia in Europe's most important institutions and ambitions. . . He outlined a program of cooperation with the European Union on Russian membership in the World Trade Organization. Putin also advanced a promising dialogue nurtured by NATO Secretary General George Robertson by imagining out loud that NATO membership for the Baltic states and *eventually for Russia* could contribute to stability in Europe" (emphasis mine).

In a remarkably informative article in the November 12 issue of the *Washington Post Weekly,* John Newhouse reports on the October 3 private conversation between Putin and the NATO Secretary General. Newhouse writes:

> The terrorist threat laid bare on Sept. 11 is transforming global security arrangements. . . Putin's broad purpose—to link his ailing, self-absorbed country to the United States while moving it into the European mainstream—has been gathering force for some time. . . When he meets with Bush . . . this week, the two men can be expected to start a process aimed at moving their countries into a shifting strategic environment. And that move could edge NATO, the centerpiece of America's security relationship with Europe, to the sidelines.
>
> Well before Sept. 11, NATO was the object of some tough questions: Did it still have a purpose? Was there a role in it for Russia, and if so, how central a role? A few Western leaders, starting with Britain's Tony Blair, had in one degree

or another concluded that Western and Russian strategic interests had converged, and that collective security arrangements that lacked Russian participation no longer made sense. . . [The private conversation in Brussels] pointed up Putin's resolve to anchor Russia to the West, and the intensity of his hatred of the Taliban and radical Islam. . .

Topic A was the Russian link to NATO. Neither man saw any reason Russia shouldn't be a member. . . [Robertson] also raised the idea of a conference on military responses to terrorism jointly sponsored by NATO and Russia, an idea Putin liked. . . [Russia's concern about NATO expansion] becomes moot as [Putin] moves to acquire a serious role in revised Western security arrangements and to segue into Europe on his own.

The *Wall Street Journal* reported in its November 12 issue:

Mr. Putin, who leaves today for Washington, told U.S. media organizations gathered in the Kremlin on Saturday that the Sept. 11 attacks had shown [that the U.S. and Russia] must escape "Cold War cliches" and rally together to defeat what he described as their common terrorist foe. . . Mr. Putin . . . stressed repeatedly that a "new dimension" in relations rests on a shared desire to see terrorism "destroyed, eliminated, and liquidated." . . .

[Putin spoke of] his goal of securing the U.S. as a "reliable and stable partner." Referring to the threat of terrorism, he said: "It is quite obvious to any objective observer today that we could find an effective response to these challenges only if we [Russia, the U.S. and other key allies] put our efforts together. We can do that if we raise the level of mutual confidence, of mutual trust to a new level and raise the quality to a new level."

This is a very strong series of statements from a man known for choosing his words carefully.

The November 12 issue of the *Los Angeles Times* observed: "Putin quickly signed on to the U.S.-led counterterrorism coalition because it addressed an issue dear to his heart: collective security." The *Times* also reported in its November 14 issue: "In a joint statement, the two presidents said the former adversaries now have "a new relationship . . . founded on a commitment to the values of democracy, the free market and the rule of law. The United States and Russia have overcome the legacy of the Cold War. Neither country regards the other as an enemy or threat." And in its November 19 issue: "Putin's support for the [anti-terrorism] campaign has been accompanied by efforts to bring Russia closer to Western economic and security organizations [meaning: the EU, WTO, NATO]."

George F. Will, writing in the November 26 issue of *Newsweek,* observed: "Last week Vladimir Putin, visiting the United States, gave additional evidence that the force of the explosions at the World Trade Center and the Pentagon may have blown Russia into Europe."

A Russian-NATO alliance would not likely be feasible if NATO were to remain a *military organization.* This would promise to be too cumbersome. But if NATO, as President Putin himself has suggested, were to transform from a military into a political organization, neither Europe nor Russia would have legitimate cause for overwhelming resistance. The admission of Russia into a transformed NATO would result in a political reconciliation of the civilization that formally divided into eastern and western branches in the year 1054.

My argument here is that a U.S./British/Russian military alliance could be formed *outside of NATO* yet operate in a close political affiliation *with NATO*. All three nations would belong to both alliances. The global enforcement capacities of this set of alliances would be well beyond anything the freedom-resisting governments of the world could effectively challenge.

The U.S. and Russia have every good reason, from historical cultural affinities to common defense imperatives, to form a comprehensive military and political alliance. The common need for both countries is a far-reaching set of military and diplomatic decisions, from the removal of Saddam Hussein to the destruction of the theological concepts of the Islamic militants. The combined resources of the U.S., Britain, and Russia would produce an alliance capable of transforming the global architecture and removing the threats that currently confront us.

An aggressive and finely calculated nuclear posture by such a Triple Alliance would promise to stagger the psychology of opposition among the governments resisting the consensus of freedom, progress, and equality. As to the support base of the terrorists, it could do nothing but melt away once the terms of competition had been raised to a level beyond the engagement capacity of the Crescent, and, in fact, beyond its current ability to imagine.

It could be argued that such a measure would provoke other nuclear-equipped nations to then justify the use of their own atomic weapons (such as India and Pakistan, or North Korea if it actually has them). I do not believe this argument would be consistent with the facts of human nature or of international realpolitik. A displayed willingness of a northern

Triple Alliance to use nuclear weapons in the face of threats would vastly reduce the willingness of other nations to even indicate a threatening posture. The enforcement capabilities of such an alliance, once it had already demonstrated a willingness to strike with its ultimate weapons, would be sufficient to negotiate an actual reduction in the number of nations possessing a nuclear arsenal. Under the influence of adequate persuasion, and in return for generous and concrete favors and guarantees, nations such as Pakistan and India could be prevailed upon to give up their small nuclear arsenals and dismantle their production capacities. If the number of nuclear-equipped nations were reduced to the U.S., Britain, Russia, France, China, and Israel, the club could be closed and any attempts at new membership answered with overwhelming severity. Such a nuclear-enforced world order would seem to be the only possible means of maintaining any order at all in an age of mass travel and proliferating knowledge.

An American/British/Russian military alliance would liberate us from our hostage status to the vexatious "coalition" that our government has been jockeying to maintain. This current coalition is a distraction to our focus and a drag on our mobility. Robert Kagan, in the October 22 issue of the *Post Weekly,* made the following observations: "It's important to have partners in this struggle. But a little sober realism is in order, too. At the end of the day, there is a limited number of nations we can trust to look out for our most vital interests, and an even smaller number strong enough and stable enough to be of real help. . . But if we let the coalition of the unwilling call the shots, they'll gladly drag us down to defeat, everywhere."

Although we may be able to sustain this awkward coalition for the remainder of our military operation in Afghanistan, we are being unanimously warned by Arab leaders that an attack on Iraq, or on any Arab nation, will explode the coalition and possibly send the situation in the Middle East spiraling out of control. The repressive Arab governments are terrified of this, and rightly so. These governments are not friends to freedom, and they are not friends to us. Neither are they friends to the millions of Muslims whom they terrorize in their own countries. This coalition is dispensable, as well as the belief that we are dependent on Saudi Arabian oil. A recent article in the *Wall Street Journal* emphasized this in its caption, *We Do Not Need Saudi Arabia's Oil.*

The current coalition of dubious and utterly untrustworthy governments will consistently attempt to paralyze our overall effort. OPEC's heated attempt to coordinate a significant cutback in oil production, and thereby hammer the already struggling Western economies by a spike in oil prices, has been offset almost single-handedly by one of our few true allies in this campaign to liquidate Islamic terrorism. That ally is Russia, the third biggest oil-exporting country in the world (with vastly more undeveloped potential). After Saudi Arabia and Iran, the countries exporting the most oil worldwide are Russia, Norway, Venezuela, and Mexico. The combined daily output of these four countries is almost sixteen million barrels, over twenty percent of what the entire world produces. Oil in the Middle East is, of course, critical to the world oil supply and to the stability of the world economy. But a *temporary disruption* in the flow from that region would not cripple us if we were to secure alternative sources ahead of such an event (and the disruption would be only temporary if it did occur). President Putin has assured us that his country is willing to provide much of that alternative source. The *Los Angeles Times* reported on November 15: "[President Putin] mingled with cowboy capitalists Wednesday, seeking their investments and touting the two countries' shared interest in Russia's vast oil fields. . . [He] referred to his country as 'reliable and predictable partner' in supplying oil and gas. . . . Putin said it would benefit Russia and the United States to cooperate on energy matters. Because the United States is eager to reduce its dependence on oil from the politically uncertain Middle East, Russia's reserves are increasingly attractive to Texas oil companies."

The November 12 issue of the *Wall Street Journal* reported:

> President Vladimir Putin, outlining high hopes for a summit this week with President Bush, says Russia seeks a new partnership with its former Cold War foe that would reshape 30-year-old arms-control rules, promote joint action against terrorism and boost Russia's role as an alternative source of energy. . . Mr. Putin offered Russia as a long-term supplier of oil and gas amid concerns that instability could disrupt shipments from the Middle East.
>
> The world economy, he said, needs to "diversify its energy supplies and diversify risk. . . Russia is very suited to this." Russia is the world's third-largest oil producer, behind Saudi Arabia and the U.S. [Note to reader: do not confuse "exporter" with "producer."]

Newsweek reported in its November 26 issue: "Russia, Putin noted, is pumping oil at a furious rate, helping the world economy by undermining OPEC's effort to raise prices." In the event of a temporary cutback in the flow of Middle Eastern oil, Russia, Norway, and the Western Hemisphere have plenty of oil to provide for Euro-American needs in the interim.

U.S. and British oil companies, as Mr. Putin acknowledges, are needed for an optimal expansion of the production of oil in Russia. A large-scale investment in Russia by the Western oil industry, accompanied by a Russian commitment to substantially develop its legal institutions for the promotion and safeguarding of a truly modern market economy, would be a giant step forward in Putin's effort to comprehensively develop the Russian economy and democracy.

With a Russian commitment to deepen and expand its legal infrastructure, Putin's country holds out the promise of a gargantuan boomtown for foreign investment. The November 16 issue of the *Los Angeles Times* reported on Putin's one-hour appearance on an American radio talk show: "During an unprecedented hour of questioning Thursday night . . . Putin plunged into American talk radio—showing off his dry wit and his contempt for terrorists, expressing optimism about the future of democracy in his country. . . Putin said that the main barrier to a free press in Russia is the immaturity of the country's market economy, which keeps the media beholden to their financial sponsors. But he said that he's confident that the market economy and democracy in Russia are continuing in parallel paths. 'This is an irreversible process,' [Putin testified]. 'The foundation of the democracy will continue to strengthen, and the market economy will continue to progress. . . The point of no return is way in the past.'"

These are not the words of a person with a diluted commitment to democracy, to the rule of law, and to an efficient open-market system. Although I am certain Mr. Putin has his own agenda, and am by no means recommending an unqualified confidence in the motives and aims of the current leader of Russia, my point is that Russia's president is far too intelligent to fail to recognize the imperatives of the day. If his country is to reverse its decline, and if Russia is to have any hope of maintaining a dominant world presence throughout the twenty-first century, it must aggressively pursue its political and economic transition. It must also obtain history's testimony that Russia played a leading role in removing the presence of Islamic militancy from the face of the earth.

At home, in the presence of opposition among the elite to his reach toward the West, Putin's hand would be strengthened by a massive influx of direct foreign investment by American and European companies. Banking, accounting, construction, green technologies, and virtually every major business category are promising spheres of investment for Westerners eager to assist the Russians in building a solid democracy and a vibrant economy. To assist the Russians in negotiating this transition into a full-blown political democracy with a successful open market must be one of the dominant foreign policy objectives for the United States at the present time.

In the November 12 issue of the *Los Angeles Times,* Robin Wright quoted "a senior State Department official": "Putin is looking for a whole bunch of signs, not to convince him, but to convince the folks back home . . . that the United States now thinks of Russia as a Western country. . . And we understand too that *the more we show Russia's future is in the West, the more it will head in that direction*—and will embrace the kind of democratic and economic reforms that will show it is *one of us*" (emphasis mine). But the tangible element—Russia's national pride—is all the more critical.

Until early in the last decade, the poor and struggling Russian people enjoyed considerable psychological satisfaction in the world-class status of their country. On a par with the United States, they had dominated global politics since the end of World War II. With the breakup of the Soviet Union, and the collapse of the Russian economy in the fledgling transition from a central command to a free and open system, the status of "global superpower" was lost. A majority of Russians have remained as poor under capitalism as they had been under communism. But they have the added indignities of no reliable social security (as they at least had enjoyed under the communist model) and the humiliation of seeing the United States trumpeted as "the world's only remaining superpower." This is particularly galling to the military leadership, which knows that Russia is still a *military* superpower (although it has been unable to defeat the tiny and poorly armed Chechen resistance forces). An imperative for President Putin, if he is to maintain the support of the Russian elite in his effort to transform the country into a mature democracy with a liberal market system, is to restore the global prestige that Russia has lost over the past ten years.

In its November 16 issue, the *Los Angeles Times* reported: "[In Russia, 18 former generals and admirals] criticized Putin's plans to downsize the military and close its bases [in Cuba and Vietnam], which symbolized Russian aspirations to remain a global military power. . . [A hardline Russian newspaper said of Putin and President Bush]: 'Bush represents the countries that are headed toward global hegemony, while Putin represents a country in full retreat.'"

In the *Times'* November 13 issue, Robert E. Hunter observed: "The ABM treaty now mostly matters to Russia as a symbol of its still being taken seriously as a major power."

Membership in a Triple Alliance with the U.S. and Britain, along with a seat among the leading members of NATO, would restore to Russia the status and the sense of prestige it had lost since it abandoned the communist model.

A coordinated nuclear strike on the most exalted spiritual landmarks of the militants would serve an ultimate notice to our enemies, and it would catapult Russia into a position of world-class dominance and prestige. I believe the Russians would be willing to consent to our use of nuclear weapons in ending the war on terrorism if Russia itself became an equal participant in the peacemaking mission.

Addendum to Article Ten

The November 26 issue of *Newsweek* described a remarkable scene during the Bush-Putin summit: "In the living-room, Bush sat for his national-security briefing with CIA Director George Tenet. Bush asked his pal 'Vladimir'—who'd spent 16 years in the KGB—to sit in."

A former head of the KGB was invited to a national-security briefing of a U.S. president whose father had been the head of the CIA. If nothing else, we can all agree "the times have changed." David S. Broder wrote for the October 22 issue of the *Washington Post Weekly:* "It was this president's father who used that phrase [New World Order] to characterize the post-Cold War international system, but George H.W. Bush was never able to give much content to those words. Now the pace and scale of change are so awesome that leaders and people alike are being called on to construct whole new frameworks of thought and analysis."

Our new president has told us little, if anything, about what he sees for the direction of our nation and the structure of the world beyond our inevitable victory in this war against terrorism. A *Newsweek* article from the November 26 issue lamented: "[President Bush has yet] to articulate a vision for the world that he's shaping with Putin and Britain's Tony Blair."

Our president is an efficient administrator, yet he can hardly be called a visionary. Soon after his swearing-in, when asked to state the dominant vision that would inspire his administration, he answered: "Tax relief." A commendable objective, but hardly a broad vision for our nation and its evolving relationship with world history. Yet we have watched this same president grab a bull by its horns and pledge a fight to the death. And we believe his pledge. Whether we liked him or not, he is the man of the hour and history itself has climbed on his shoulders. Our responsibility is to support him in whatever fashion or degree we are each capable of. At the present moment, this is what it means to be an American.

Whatever the vision, or the lack thereof, in the mind of our president at this moment, he has made it clear that Vladimir Putin and Tony Blair, and the formidable nations they lead, will be his crucial allies as history is carried, gun in hand, from today into tomorrow.

11.   The Role of Israel

After Britain and Russia, in this current contest we have no ally more important than Israel. We should bring Israel into the coalition, and open the door wide for all who want to leave.

I am not a fan of Ariel Sharon, and my views on numerous issues relating to the nation of Israel would not find support among a majority of the people of that nation. I am neither an anti-Semite nor a philo-Semite. I am an American with an ambitious eye for the security interests of my country and for the betterment of the welfare of human beings in general—regardless of race, class, or nationality.

Whatever one's views on the issues relating to Israel, any serious discussion on global security arrangements has to reckon with the realities in Palestine. The problems in that land have an inflammatory role in what has effectively become a war that encompasses the globe.

Although the dilemma in Palestine is not the major grievance of the international terrorists, this dilemma is a dominant source of propaganda in the fueling of Islamic hostilities, not only in the Middle East and Far East, but also among Muslim communities in Europe and America.

In an October article in the *Los Angeles Times*, W. Scott Thompson described an e-mail from a U.S.-educated Muslim couple in Indonesia on September 11: "When we heard the news from New York, we broke out a bottle of champagne. . . It served you right—supporting that terrorist . . . Sharon."

Our relationship with Israel has led Muslims throughout the world to so identify us with Israel that Jew haters celebrated the September 11 massacres as though it were Israel itself that had been attacked. L. Paul Bremer wrote in the September 13 issue of the *Journal:* "Mr. Arafat and his colleagues have created an environment that made possible the spectacle of schoolchildren in Gaza cheering the news [of September 11]."

Until the problem in Palestine is decisively resolved, the psychological strength of the Islamic terrorist movement will retain a principal source of its energy.

A careful study of the history of the Jewish/Arab dilemma in Palestine leads to the realization that there is no end of the list of grievances on either side. Years ago, when reading a pro-Palestinian article, I would find myself feeling a measure of indignation toward the Israeli government. This would last until my next reading of a pro-Israeli article, which would induce within me a measure of indignation toward the leadership of the Palestinians. Back and forth I went, wrestling in my conscience and in my intellect for an adequate view of the situation—one that I could justify to myself convincingly on the basis of a fair and comprehensive survey of the data. Eventually I concluded it is likely impossible to properly organize the data so as to form a truly educated opinion on this level of analysis. The list of grievances on each side goes on forever. For each allegation there is a counter-allegation, immediately answered by a counter-counter-allegation, and so on ad infinitum. All the while, the funerals continue.

What if we dismissed, as a frame of reference, the endless lists of grievances, and introduced a new set of concepts around which to organize our thoughts?

The guiding principle in our foreign policy today is the war on terrorism. The organizing philosophy in this war (at least, according to our government's official position) is spelled out in our president's oft-repeated formula: "Our enemy is a radical network of terrorists, and every government that supports them."

Throughout the Middle East and beyond, the terrorists' hatred of the Jews has merged with a hatred of America in an escalating feedback relationship. It is now, as a psychological fact, out of control. We should keep in mind that Hitler too had legitimate grievances. The evil of Hitler's method of addressing those grievances destroyed the overall credibility of the German position, so much so that any potential concern we might have had for their grievances was eclipsed by the threat that the Nazis posed to our security and the stability of the world. Today, the greatest threat to our security and to world stability is the terrorist mass movement, which is pledged not only to the extinction of Israel but also to the extinction of America.

The debate over who has the more compelling lists of grievances in Palestine has no foreseeable outcome. The debates and the negotiations could go on forever. But the most immediate issue confronting us is not the question of which side has the preponderant legal and moral advantage. The urgent and overriding concern is the fact that Israel's most dangerous enemies see us as them. Since this is undeniably the case, we should organize our thinking around the fact that the murderers who want to destroy Israel (regardless of the merit or demerit of their grievances) also want to destroy the United States of America. If Israel's most dangerous enemies see us as them, then those enemies of Israel are the enemies of the United States. *Israel* is not that.

In a *Wall Street Journal Europe* article on July 12, after Palestinians had kidnapped and hanged two Jewish men, Alex Safian reported on a sermon by Palestinian Sheik Ahmad Abu Halabaya, broadcast live from a Gaza City mosque: "Have no mercy on the Jews no matter where they are, in any country. Fight them, wherever you are. Wherever you meet them, kill them. Wherever you are, kill those Jews and those Americans who are like them—and those who stand by them."

The Palestinian terrorists, whom Arafat's government has never shown any sincerity or consistency in confronting, are obsessed with murdering Americans as well as

Jews. As a nation, this should serve as the controlling term in our approach to the situation in Palestine. Grievances can be discussed in a time of luxury, not during a fight to the death with mass murderers who want to destroy us.

Arafat is the head of a community that harbors terrorists who have pledged themselves and the name of their god to the indiscriminate killing of Americans: "Wherever you meet them, kill them. Wherever you are, kill those Jews and those Americans who are like them."

The "Bojinka" terrorist plan, exposed through a freak accident in Manila in 1995, came replete with a manifesto describing the motives of the terrorists. The *Washington Post Weekly* provided an excerpt from this manifesto in its October 1 issue. The excerpt read: "The U.S. government gives military aircraft to the Jewish state so the Jews can continue fighting and killing. All of this is a result of the U.S. government's financial and military support of the Jewish state. All people who support the U.S. government are our target." (Osama bin Laden later included all U.S. taxpayers in his fatwa, since by their taxes they are supporting the U.S. government.) This particular terrorist plot, broken up by authorities at an advanced stage of preparation, involved the bombing of *eleven* in-flight commercial airliners in the United States, and also the hijacking and crashing of an airliner into the CIA's headquarters in Virginia.

The *Post Weekly,* in its October 15 issue, provided excerpts from the 1999 trial of Ahmad Ibrahim al Naggar, the leader of Egyptian Islamic Jihad (until his execution after the trial): "[Attacks on the United States are part of] a guerrilla warfare against Israeli and American interests not only in Arab and Muslim countries but everywhere in the world." Ahmad also testified: "Bin Laden believed that the Jewish lobby pulled the ropes of politics in the United States and was behind the weakening of Muslim people and governments, and that this hegemony should be broken."

The terrorists believe, and they act upon this belief, that the United States government is controlled by pro-Israeli, anti-Islamic Jews. This is nonsense, of course, but it is what the terrorists, including many of their sympathizers in America and Europe, believe. The most dangerous enemies of Israel see us as them, and they act with deadly force upon this perception.

On November 24, the military leader of Hamas was executed by Israeli special forces. Hamas is a violent terrorist organization financed primarily by wealthy Saudi Arabians and by the government of Iran. Their stated aim is to destroy Israel and establish an Islamic state throughout the whole of Palestine (but this is only a phase in their broader theocratic vision). As a matter of doctrinal principle, they reject even the concept of negotiation. Their political leader, Mahmoud al-Zahar, has stated in the plainest conceivable words that his organization will not call off the killing until every Jew has been eliminated from Palestine. The Hamas military leader killed on November 24, Mahmoud Abu Hanoud, had been the mastermind behind attacks such as the suicide bombing that killed twenty teenage Israelis outside a disco in Tel Aviv last summer. The *Los Angeles Times* reported in its November 25 issue: "Abu Hanoud had become a folk hero to many Palestinians." The *Times* article described the funeral procession: "Massive crowds of militants, many waving the green banners of Hamas . . . accompanied Abu Hanoud's body from the morgue in Jenin to Nablus and later to his village for burial. Tens of thousands more marched through the streets of Gaza City, also chanting for revenge." A Hamas political leader, Abdulaziz Rantisi, promised: "There will be another Abu Hanoud, and thousands of Abu Hanouds."

Six days later, twenty-five Israelis were blown to pieces by Hamas suicide bombers. The December 2 issue of the *Times* reported:

> On a night when downtown Jerusalem teems with young people, two Palestinians strode past a row of packed cafes late Saturday, then blew themselves up moments and yards apart. At least 12 people were killed . . . and more than 170 wounded. . . A car bomb exploded about 20 minutes later less than a block away as emergency crews attempted to rescue victims from the initial blasts. People fled in panic as dozens of ambulances careened throughout downtown streets.
>
> Badly mangled bodies were strewn in Zion Square, site of one explosion, and on the pavement outside the Rimon Café just off Ben Yehuda Street, where the other suicide bomber struck. . . Among the many wounded who flooded area hospitals, 11 were listed in critical condition. The majority of the casualties were Israelis in their teens or 20s.

These first two bombers killed a dozen Jews enjoying a peaceful evening in Jerusalem. Twelve hours later, the third bomber struck, killing fifteen passengers on a bus in Haifa.

Three suicide bombers. Three more folk heroes for the Palestinian necropolis of suicide-murderers. Seventy-five percent of all Palestinian Muslims support these mass murders of Jews and, if the bomber happens to be lucky, an American as a fat bonus. Jews, Americans—it's all the same to them now.

A November 18 article in the *Los Angeles Times* observed: "Taken together, the radical Hamas movement and Islamic Jihad, for the first time, have overtaken Fatah

[Arafat's party] in terms of public support."

While the Palestinian government attempts to remain covert in its support of the internationally backed terrorists operating in Palestine, the Arab society that Arafat governs is *overt* in its support of these terrorists.

Today it is the land of Israel drinking the blood of its people. Since the killers dream of someday carrying their campaign to the cities of America (and we can no longer reasonably deny this), is it rational for us to waffle or to give only lukewarm support to the reliable ally confronting these terrorists on the front lines of the war?

Another Palestinian terrorist organization is the Palestinian Islamic Jihad, which has been named by the U.S. State Department as a global terrorist organization. Islamic Jihad members openly gather, parade, and demonstrate in the areas governed by the Palestinian Authority.

On November 26, President Bush repeated and expanded his warning to the world: "If anyone harbors a terrorist, they're terrorists. If they house terrorists, they're terrorists." In the October 26 issue of the *Wall Street Journal,* Benjamin Netanyahu quoted an earlier statement by President Bush: "From this day forward, any nation that continues to support terrorism will be regarded by the United States as a hostile regime."

I wish to emphasize our president's words: "*Any* nation that continues to support terrorism will be regarded by the U.S. as a hostile regime."

As we waged our campaign against Germany and its allies sixty years ago, someone might have challenged: "We have no problem with the German people. The German people are good people."

While there would have been a substantial measure of truth in those words, we would not have succeeded had we operated from that point of view. We won that war by means of ferocious military measures. We did not hesitate to firebomb *entire city blocks*. Because the Nazi philosophy was the dominant consensus in Germany, and Germany itself was incapable of destroying the Nazi vision, it became our moral responsibility to destroy Germany. As a general rule, we did not do more than was necessary. But more importantly, we did not do less than was necessary.

With seventy-five percent of all Palestinian Muslims supporting the suicide-murderers, and given the display of jubilation among the Palestinian masses on September 11 (witnessed with our own eyes), we have no reasonable justification for failing to view the Palestinians as a terrorist community. It is true that many individuals among the Palestinians do not support the terrorists, just as many individuals among the Germans did not support the Nazis. Since Germany itself could not or would not rein in the Nazis, it became the obligation of the civilized nations to destroy Germany—notwithstanding the legitimate German grievances that had existed for two decades prior to the War. The response of the civilized nations to the Nazi-controlled German nation was morally and existentially necessary. A very similar situation now exists with regard to the terrorist-controlled Palestinian community.

At this stage in history, we are confronted with overwhelming evidence that any diplomatically negotiated peace settlement in Palestine could be *only* superficial and temporary. A straightforward survey of the fundamental beliefs and commitments of each party should have assured us long ago that, *as a matter of principle,* an ultimate showdown is inevitable.

I believe a peaceful arrangement in Palestine is possible, but not until America is willing to recognize the level at which the situation must be addressed. Although the Palestinian effort is presented through the media as a nationalist movement, at its root it is truly a religious movement. While Yasser Arafat is a terrorist leader in the vein of a

Saddam Hussein rather than an Ayatollah Khomeini, the Muslims of Hamas and Islamic Jihad are militant fundamentalists. Our government has not done a good job at helping Americans understand the difference. The Islamic militants in Palestine do not respect the concept of nationalism, although they are currently exploiting this concept for public relations advantages, and as a steppingstone toward their ultimate goal. Manuel Castells explains in *The Power of Identity* (Volume II of his Trilogy, *The Information Age: Economy, Society, and Culture,* Blackwell Publishers, 1997): "Islamic identity is reconstructed by fundamentalists in opposition to capitalism, to socialism, and to *nationalism,* Arab or otherwise, which are, in their view, all failing ideologies of the post-colonial order" (p. 17, emphasis mine). On the same page, Castells quotes from Article 10 of the Iranian Constitution: "All Muslims form a single nation."

The militants of Palestine, while shrouding their true aims in nationalist rhetoric so as to lure sympathizers to their cause (most emphatically from among the vast anti-Semitic reservoir in Europe), actually have no intention of ever stopping at the creation of a Palestinian Islamic state. As Islamic militants, they belong to the international movement that seeks to transform the surface of the earth into a single caliphate. The militants of Palestine have no less of an appetite for destroying American and European civilization than they do for destroying Israel. Since Israel will not go away, there will be no possibility of peace in Palestine until the terrorist community is confronted at the source of its confidence.

The spark that set off the current intifada was the visit by Ariel Sharon, in September 2000, to what the Jews call the Temple Mount. This place, where the Jewish temple once stood, is now the location of the Al Aqsa Mosque and the Dome of the Rock, two of the most spiritually invested structures in the entire civilization of Islam. The terrorist-controlled Palestinian community is a hotbed of the extremism that began raging in the 1970s, and an Article of Confession among all Islamic extremists is the obliteration of Israel. The principal source of the Palestinian's confidence that Israel can be exterminated is the spiritual landmark that dominates the skyline of Jerusalem. This spiritual landmark, which for many centuries has usurped the site on which the Jewish temple stood, testifies to the collective psyche of the terrorist community that their god will bless their efforts to purge the land of Palestine. So long as this landmark remains in existence, the terrorist-controlled Palestinian community will fight to the last man, woman, and child in its religiously inspired effort to drive Israel into the sea.

If the Israeli government were to *talk* of removing this landmark, the talk would provoke an outrage beyond anyone's means of controlling. But if, rather than talking at all, they were to suddenly and swiftly destroy the landmark, and quickly rebuild their own on precisely the spot where the other now stands, they would obliterate the psychological momentum and confidence of the Palestinian terrorist movement. If this action were to be synchronized with a U.S.-led erasure of the spiritual landmarks in Saudi Arabia, and the rapid elimination of the regime of Saddam Hussein, I cannot imagine what would remain of the terrorists' confidence in the purpose of Allah to destroy America.

The terrorists attach a great deal of significance to landmarks. The orgy of celebration indulged by the Palestinian community on September 11 was an expression of their belief that Allah had commenced a program that would eventuate in the collapse of American civilization (as the government-sponsored Egyptian media had announced). The obliteration of the towers in New York City, and the successful penetration of the Pentagon, was interpreted by them as a spiritual signal of the beginning of America's demise at the hands of warriors faithful to Allah. The spiritual momentum of the Islamic terrorist movement cannot now be reversed by anything short of a swift and permanent removal of the spiritual landmarks that inspire this movement (all that we are currently doing would need to continue, but this would be supplemental to the central strategy). By robbing the militants of their confidence in the favor and the purpose of Allah, we will have swiftly accomplished what our "patient accumulation of successes" never will.

We can certainly acknowledge that such a measure would be unfair to the Muslims who do not support the terrorists. We can also acknowledge that our destruction of Germany was unfair to the many Germans who did not support the Nazis. Yet since Islamic civilization itself either cannot or will not rein in the terrorists, we need offer no apologies for acting, out of moral and existential necessity, in a measure that will address the terrorist problem at its generative source. We would have no pleasure in executing such a strategy, and we could wish for a viable alternative measure, but the elimination of this threat to our security is a necessity that should override our concern for the religious sensitivities of a well-intentioned people. In an imperfect and dangerous world, we cannot always have the best of everything, and the requirements of the current situation are such that we will not have victory over the terrorists until we address their concept of God.

Until we are willing (since we are very well able) to take our enemy hostage at this level, I cannot imagine how, apart from the unacceptable alternative of genocide, we could ever succeed in eliminating the threat of mass destruction of Americans at the hands of Islamic murderers.

It is now clear, beyond any legitimate doubt, that when Arafat negotiated, his aim was to manipulate world opinion rather than to achieve a peace settlement with Israel. In truth, he will settle for nothing less than a withdrawal of the Jews from all of Palestine. His acknowledgment, in 1988, of Israel's "right to exist" was obviously a political ploy to garner support from the West and to transfer his terrorist headquarters from Tunisia into Palestine.

The most that Israel can reasonably give is far less than what Arafat will ever settle for. Except in abstract theory and in rosy scenarios, there is no actual window of opportunity on the diplomatic level (at least, there has been none in the past and there is none in the foreseeable future). Since there is no point in further negotiations with the Palestinian Authority, why continue granting diplomatic recognition? This is pure political hubris that distracts from what the situation actually requires.

Arafat himself is a prototype terrorist with a long record of bloody attacks dating back over thirty years. Netanyahu wrote in his article for the *Journal:* "Yasser Arafat is perhaps the only leader in the world who is both directly responsible for terror and whose regime also harbors terrorists. . . Hamas and Islamic Jihad, whose suicide bombings have killed and wounded hundreds of Israeli civilians since the peace process began, operate with impunity in Palestinian-controlled areas."

Although the Palestinians are not formally a nation, they are a heavily armed and organized community under the political leadership of Yasser Arafat and his Palestinian Authority. Two known terrorist organizations with international backing, Hamas and Islamic Jihad, who have called not only for the extinction of Israel but also for the indiscriminate murder of Americans, are heroes by the dominant consensus of the Palestinian people. Hamas and Islamic Jihad openly gather and march and demonstrate in areas under the political control of the Palestinian Authority, to cheering crowds of Palestinians. Whatever their grievances against the Jews might be, at the present time these grievances should be viewed as irrelevant. The Palestinian community has joined in the war of terrorism *against the United States.* Western leaders ought to stop quacking whenever Arafat tosses a crumb. He is our enemy and he always will be.

Israel is fighting Hamas and Islamic Jihad on the front lines of this war. It is neither in the interests of our security nor in the service of our national integrity to pressure Israel for military restraint. This is not a time for diplomacy. It is a day of war.

In his *Journal* article, Netanyahu proceeds to adroitly touch on a fact that is causing increasing discomfort and even embarrassment for many Americans (as is evident from letters to editors throughout America, and in commentaries from both the Left and the Right): "But rather than unequivocally supporting Israel in its battle against a terrorist regime, many voices in the free world have called on Israel to make concessions to the Palestinian Authority."

Our president has articulated a Doctrine to guide us in this war with an enemy every bit as evil and every bit as insane as the Nazis. How do Yasser Arafat, and those whom he represents, merit even a partial exemption from this Doctrine? Is the Doctrine a matter of principle or merely a shifting political posture? Will the current governing administration of the United States be labeled by history as the leader of the effort to destroy terrorism or as the administration that equivocated in its support of an ally fighting this war on the front lines with its back to the wall?

In the effort to hold together this burdensome coalition, our government has created a perception (I am not suggesting it is accurate, but a real and escalating perception nonetheless) that we are equivocating in the support of our most faithful friend and valuable ally outside of Europe. The following exchange between a reporter and a State Department spokesman illustrates the growing vexation over the government's lukewarm and equivocal support of

Israel in its front-line war against Islamic terrorism:

> State Department spokesman Philip Reeker:
> "We oppose a policy of targeted killings [of
> Islamic terrorists in Palestine by the Israeli mili-
> tary]. . ."
> Question: "Can you expand on your opposi-
> tion to the policy—to the Israeli policy of tar-
> geted killings vis-à-vis U.S. policy to target
> Osama bin Laden, Mullah Omar?"
> Mr. Reeker: "I can't really draw a parallel
> between the two. Our position on the Israeli pol-
> icy of targeted killings is well known, has not
> changed since the (inaudible)."
> Question: "Why is there no parallel? Would
> it be provocative to attack Osama bin Laden and
> kill him? Would you object to that?"
> Mr. Reeker: "I don't have anything to add to
> what the president and the secretary of state and
> everyone else have said about our campaign
> against terrorism." (Quoted from the *Wall Street
> Journal,* October 18)

The searing perception of hypocrisy, fueled by sorry
public performances such as that rendered by Philip Reeker
in this instance, could eventually threaten the strong sense of
patriotism (á la the Vietnam era) and the energetic support
of our government currently strong in America. When a
president's approval rating is at ninety percent, his administration can brush off issues that cannot be ignored when that
rating inevitably drops to a less emotionally induced level.

The previously quoted article by Robert L. Pollock
is challenging in other places as well:

> President Bush spoke with great moral clarity

last month when he told Congress that America could tolerate neither terrorists nor those who harbor them. But since then the administration has refused to allow its coalition-building efforts to [be] hobbled by a foolish consistency. . . [Yasser Arafat] would certainly seem to fit the Bush definition of "those who harbor terrorists." . . . As if the assassination of a U.S. cabinet secretary would not be considered an act of war.

Indeed, the appearance of hypocrisy is increasingly raised by the Bush administration's attempts to exclude terrorists who attack Israel from the U.S.'s "war on terrorism." . . . As the Bush administration tries to adjust to these new realities [brought home to us on September 11], it would be better served by a consistent moral compass than a willingness to compromise for short-term stability or ephemeral coalitions. The path of appeasement is fraught with danger.

Arieh Greenbaum of Los Angeles wrote to the editor of the *Los Angeles Times:* "The difference [in contrast with Bin Laden] is that Arafat, by far, is more adept at fooling people. . . Both have a dangerous agenda for their respective regimes. . . Utopia would be wonderful if Arafat rally meant anything he tells his own people, that there is no room for an Israel in the Middle East?" (November 7 issue.)

I believe Israel is more important to us as an ally than all of the Arab nations combined. Israel has, by far, the most disciplined and powerful military in the Middle East. In terms of "bang for the buck," Israel has the most efficient military/intelligence apparatus in the world. Their ability to penetrate and to gather sensitive information is almost frightening even to their friends. This nation, Israel, regardless of the merits and demerits of its history over the past century, has been conditioned by fire as no other nation ever has. We must *want them on our team,* not as a fringe player but as a confidante in our inner circle. This is a people we can count on. And this is a nation that has consistently demonstrated its comprehensive superiority over its enemies from Egypt to Iraq. Israel's enemies, as we learned unanswerably on September 11, are the enemies of the United States of America.

We need a coalition of genuine and powerful allies. That would be Britain and Russia in the north, with Israel and Turkey in the south.

Tunku Varadarajan made a crucial observation in the September 19 issue of the *Journal:* "There are two classes of ally among the states to which the U.S. will turn for cooperation. . . The second, truer kind of ally is the one whose support for any war on Islamic terror is not opportunistic, but instinctive and philosophical. Its fight against this terror is driven by the deepest conviction . . . and need, for not to fight would spell doom for its society, and for its civilization. . . Israel's very existence depends, daily, on combating and overcoming terror." (I should add that Mr. Varadarajan argues that India also qualifies as a "truer kind of ally" in this war. Although I agree, I cannot seriously believe India would prove reliable in the long term.)

The organizing term for our logic in approaching the Palestinian situation should be the threat of Islamic terrorism, which is supported by the Palestinians and opposed by Israel.

The Arab states will not remain in the coalition if we take military action against an Arab country. Yet if we refrain for this reason from such action against a dangerous Arab nation, we will effectively castrate our war effort and throw mud on our national integrity.

This coalition is artificial and unreliable. It is a drag

on our intellectual and physical mobility. We need a coalition of genuine and formidable allies to create and enforce a new paradigm of national and international arrangements. Israel is indispensable to such a coalition. The Arab nations are not.

12. History is the Crucible of Ideas

(Notice to the reader: Unpleasant materials are included in this Article.)

In the world, the power of an idea is tested by its success on the ground, not by its philosophical or moral consistency. "Israel" is an idea whose time is now. Israel's opponents are on the wrong side of history.

The historical succession of political systems represents, for other nations, a manifold attempt to genuinely express an inner culture. In contrast, America *is* democracy. This is our inner culture. For all of our struggles with inconsistency and apathy, the history of America is a history of democracy. If democracy is viewed as merely a historical experiment, then America itself is merely an experiment.

Prior to the founding of the United States of America, liberal democracy had existed only in concept. America is the preeminent concretization and historical testing of this concept. If the communists had conquered the world, their idea would have proven itself more powerful, at least for its time, than liberal democracy. The fact that it did not is what demonstrates the power of our idea. Philosophically, communism has much to say that sounds quite appealing: "From each according to his ability, to each according to his need!"—and many other such slogans that sound good in a storybook but do not translate effectively in the real world. Reading Marx can be a titillating intellectual experience, but human nature is violently opposed to an operational communism.

In Palestine today, the idea of *Israel* is more powerful than the ideas that oppose Israel. Those who contend for ideas that oppose Israel—such as Hamas, the Palestinian Authority, and anti-Israeli parties in other countries—are on the wrong side of history. One of the many attestations of this historical momentum of the concept *Israel* is the revolutionary change in relations between the Jews and the Russians, whose persecution of the Jews was a major stimulus in the early development of Zionism.

This change was in progress prior to September 11, as Jackson Diehl reports in the October 22 issue of the *Washington Post Weekly:* "Six days before Sept. 11, Israeli Prime Minister Ariel Sharon and Russian President Vladimir Putin—the leaders of two countries that never used to get along—met in Moscow and found one strong area of agreement: 'the danger,' as Sharon put it, 'of fundamentalist, extremist Islamic terror.' It was the beginning of what is becoming a beautiful friendship—and one of the most dangerous points of weakness within the U.S. counterterrorist alliance."

Mr. Diehl's assessment of this evolving Russian/ Jewish friendship (which is attested also by many Jews living within Russia)—that it is "one of the most dangerous points of weakness within the U.S. counterterrorist alliance"—is, of course, diametrically opposed to the position I am advancing in these eleventh and twelfth articles. My point, however, is the fact of the sea change in Russian attitudes toward Jews and the state of Israel. This also adds significantly to the accumulative testimony of the past one hundred years—that *Israel* is a geopolitical concept whose time has come, and that all opposition to this concept will fall under the weight of history.

Before thinking to lecture the ascendant nation of Israel on its policies, we might consider how America became such a vast and geographically privileged nation.

After the successful defeat of the British and the ease with which the Native Americans were being pushed farther and farther west, leading members of the United States evolved a philosophy of *manifest destiny.* By the mid-1840s, this philosophy had become an article of faith in the rising American nation. It was believed that the *destiny* of the United States was to expand, by force if necessary, to the western sea.

Beginning in the year 1821, the U.S. government began encouraging citizens to migrate and build small settlements in Texas, a large and loosely governed region of the Mexican state of Coahuila. Initially the Mexican government looked favorably upon these sparse American settlements, as the Americans industriously developed the land and provided a significant economic boost. But the settlers kept coming and coming. The number of Americans in Texas began rivaling the number of Mexicans. In December 1845, the U.S. government annexed Texas. No recompense, and no apologies. A straightforward land grab.

Soon afterward, President Polk sent a high-level envoy to offer the Mexican government a sum of money for California, Nevada, Utah, Arizona, Colorado, New Mexico, and southern Wyoming. Mexico was appalled, and expressed no interest in selling its land. The *Columbia Encyclopedia* explains: "When Mexico declined to negotiate, the United States prepared to take by force what it could not achieve by diplomacy. The war was heartily supported by the outright imperialists and by those who wished slaveholding territory extended" (p. 1761, article entitled "Mexican War," Columbia University Press, 1993).

The U.S. army deliberately provoked numerous skirmishes with Mexican forces, thereby creating a pretext for wholesale military aggression. In September 1847, U.S. troops entered Mexico City and compelled the government to negotiate a sale of the land desired by the United States. In a treaty signed in February 1848, America agreed to give Mexico $15 million for the territory that now makes up the southwestern portion of the United States.

Was this "right"? That is hardly a relevant question. Regardless of how "wrong" it was, the United States will never give back this land. The concept of "good and evil" has never been a guiding term of reference in international relations, and most emphatically in issues related to boundaries. We can offer our moral protests against the realpolitik of international relations, but we will not succeed in making "good and evil" a guiding concept in boundary issues and other major affairs between governments.

In 1795, the U.S. government persuaded the Native American tribes of Ohio to move westward. The Native American leaders signed the Treaty of Greenville, assuring them of secure borders in Indiana in exchange for their withdrawal from Ohio. Within twenty years, the United States unilaterally violated the treaty and began pressuring the Indians to move west of the Mississippi River. In 1830, President Andrew Jackson signed the Indian Removal Act, authorizing the military to forcefully resettle the Indians, whose ancestors had lived and died on this land for thousands of years. The forced relocations were traumatic, as is exemplified in the deaths of four thousand Cherokees out of the eleven thousand who were forced to migrate under harsh conditions in 1838. By the year 1860, scarcely any Indians remained east of the Mississippi.

In 1834, Congress designated parts of Kansas, Nebraska, and Oklahoma as the *Indian Territory,* but after two decades the Territory was encroached by U.S. settlers. In 1890, the U.S. Cavalry completed its breakdown of Indian resistance by the massacre in Wounded Knee. In 1907, the American land grab was finalized with the abolishing of the Indian Territory. The U.S. doctrine of Manifest Destiny was now a fact on the ground.

The land upon which this great nation was built was taken by force.

In 1973, as many of us will recall, a group of Native Americans launched a violent protest in Wounded Knee. They passionately pleased for public recognition of some three hundred treaties that the U.S. government had violated in its history of aggression against Native American Indians. Although an argument could be made that their cause is "just," the U.S. government has no intention of ever honoring those treaties.

Although the United States has accomplished an enormous amount of good in the world, provides its citizens with opportunities unequalled in other countries, and has shown international goodwill in a measure unmatched in the history of nations, our government also has a long record of intrigue, assassination, and betrayal.

We are free, if we choose, to criticize the Israeli government for its aggressive policies in Palestine. But we should keep in mind that the Israelis have granted far more concessions to the Palestinians than we did to the Native Americans or to the Mexicans. This is not to suggest that Israel is "in the right," or that it is "in the wrong." My point is that history itself is the crucible of ideas, and the question of "good or evil" will always be subordinate to the success of power in an imperfect world.

In the year 63 BC, the Roman General Pompey annexed Palestine. About 130 years later, the Romans destroyed the Temple and declared Jerusalem off-limits to Jews (up to a million Jews were killed in that war, and many others carried off as slaves to places as far away as central Europe in one direction and India in another). A second war with Rome, led by the pseudo-messianic general Bar Kochba, ended in the year 135 and resulted in the deaths of up to five hundred thousand Jews. It was the last large-scale Jewish military effort until the twentieth century. Not for the first time, a foreign nation had forcefully wrested control of Palestine from the Jewish people.

Although many thousands of Jews remained in Galilee, they were banned from the province of Judea. Jerusalem became populated by foreigners of various nationalities.

Beyond Palestine, Jewish communities sprang up throughout the Middle East, North Africa, and Europe. Wherever they migrated, they tenaciously held to their identity as expressed in obedience to the evolving model of the rabbis. This model was a rich articulation of Jewishness as understood by the rabbinic leadership. Among the cardinal points in that rabbinic doctrine were the conviction that Israel was being punished for its disobedience to the Law given through Moses, and that the Jews should not attempt to recover their heritage by human strength but rather should strive to perfect obedience and await the coming Messiah (whom, they believed, would regather them in Palestine, rebuild the Temple, and reconstitute the Jewish nation). This model provided the framework of thought within which the broadly scattered and downtrodden Jewish people elaborated and sustained a viable civilization even while they suffered dispersion throughout the world.

Although the land of Israel had been taken from them by force and was occupied by Gentiles, Jews throughout the world faithfully prayed three times each day for the recovery of their ancient homeland and the rebuilding of the Temple. Although forbidden by their own leadership from pursuing this vision by means of human strength, the recovery of their homeland remained a central and undying hope for the scattered civilization of the Jews.

Thomas A. Idinopulus describes in *Jerusalem Blessed, Jerusalem Cursed* (Ivan R. Dee, 1991, p. 94):

> [The Galilean rabbinic leadership] declared that despite the military defeats, despite the continuation of foreign occupation, Judea, Jerusalem, the whole land of Israel was to be recognized by all Jews everywhere as the center of the nation's existence. . . Mourning the loss of

the land, lamenting the exile from Jerusalem, bemoaning the destruction of the Temple—all became incorporated into the daily prayers of every Jew. . . When a man painted his house he left a portion unpainted to remind him of the incompleteness of his life with the land, Jerusalem, and the Temple. To convey the same meaning, a woman would omit a piece of her jewelry, or one course of a meal would be left out. . . The bridegroom would crush with his foot a wine goblet to remind the wedding party of the destruction of the Temple.

Century after century, the Jewish people held steadfastly to the rabbinic paradigm in the various countries among which they had been dispersed. Idinopulus explains: "The people, despite political boundaries separating them, looked upon themselves as one nation, practicing one ritual expressing a common hope of returning through God's agency [Messiah] to the ancestral land and its cherished capital" (p. 96).

From all over the world, Jewish communities would send legal questions to the rabbinic authorities in the land of Israel. Later (after the Galilean leadership was effectively subdued by the Romans), questions were submitted to the authorities at the great rabbinic academies in Babylonia (a truly decentralized system of Jewish religious leadership did not develop until the ninth and tenth centuries).

These written queries (asking for authoritative legal decisions on local issues, according to rabbinic law) would be given to a Jew, often a merchant, traveling in the direction of Palestine. If that particular traveler did not go all the way, at a certain point he would pass the query to a Jew heading further in that direction, until the query eventually reached the rabbinic leaders in Galilee or Babylonia. The authorities would render a decision and send a *responsa* back to the community that had "mailed" the query. When the *responsa* arrived, it was accepted as binding.

Early in the fifth century, about 350 years after the formal expulsion of the Jews from Jerusalem, a church leader named Jerome routinely observed the Jews paying bribes to enter the city and weep over its destruction. He wrote: "Silently they come and silently they go, weeping they come and weeping they go. . . That they may weep over the ruins of their state, they pay a price [bribes to the officials] . . . so that not even weeping is free to them. . . A crowd of pitiable creatures assembles . . . they weep over the ruins of the Temple; and yet they are not worthy of pity. Thus they lament on their knees . . . while the guards demand their reward for permitting them to shed some more tears" (Idinopulus, pp. 100–101).

Relations between the Jews and other Gentile neighbors, both in Palestine and abroad, were generally noneventful during the first two centuries following the second Jewish-Roman War. This began to change, in Christianized lands, during the second half of the fourth century. By the middle of the fifth century, within the far-reaching Roman Empire a series of laws had been passed that aimed at degrading the economic and social status of the Jewish people. The practical effect of these discriminatory laws and policies was to profile the Jew as an object of contempt among the general population, which led inevitably to progressive abuse. The destruction of synagogues and the plundering of Jewish possessions by Christian mobs became commonplace.

As Jews were gradually forced out of agriculture (by their being forbidden to own land, and by legislation restricting their ability to hire workers), they cultivated urban skills such as manufacturing and shop ownership. Their success led to legislation discouraging their continuance in these vocations, and left many Jews with little option other than a career in finance. Since the Christians, as a general rule, were averse to such a vocation due to their fear of offending God by "the love of money," the Jews took the lead in developing methods of using money to multiply money. They did this, not primarily or necessarily as a matter of greed, but rather of existential necessity.

In the sixth century, the Western Goths (Visigoths) of Spain were converted to Catholic Christianity. The first Catholic Spanish King, Reccared, decreed a ban on the holding of public office by a Jew, and ordered that all children born of intermarriage must be baptized. From 587 to 711, a series of Visigothic kings, with three brief exceptions, escalated the hostile campaign against the Spanish Jews. Many Jews submitted to mandatory baptism yet remained "secret Jews," and many others chose torture, death, or expulsion from land their ancestors had lived and died on for centuries. In 631, King Sisenand increased the "Jew tax" and decreed that all Jewish converts caught secretly observing Judaism were to be legally classified as permanent slaves, along with their descendants. In 652, Receswinth introduced a law forbidding the emigration of forced converts, as the flight of Jews was hurting the tax and labor base in Spain. Under Erwig, beginning in 680, the punishment for conviction as a secret Jew was increased to a choice of one hundred lashes or scalping. Under Egica in 694, Jewish children over six years of age were taken from their parents and raised in Christian homes, and the parents sold into permanent slavery.

Relief in Spain arrived with the Muslim invasion of the eighth century.

In 638, the Arab Muslims had conquered Palestine and later built magnificent mosques on the site where the Jewish temple once stood. The building of Islamic shrines on the Temple site was a traumatic experience for the Jews worldwide. However, under the Arab occupation of the ancient Jewish homeland, the Jews were treated much better than during the occupation by the Romans and Byzantines (rulers of the eastern division of the Roman Empire). In 711, the Muslims crossed the Straits of Gibraltar and killed the last Visigothic king, Roderic. For the next three centuries, the Spanish Jews participated with the Arab Muslims in a remarkable cultural episode in Spanish history. Although the Jews remained second-class citizens and were resented by a majority of the poorer Muslims, they openly excelled in various fields and made enormous contributions to the wealth, administration, and overall success of Spain during the reign of the Arabs. The Jewish situation deteriorated with the eleventh century invasion of Spain by fanatical, racially mixed Muslims from North Africa (the "Berbers," or "Moors," from the Barbary Coast/Morocco).

During the Visigothic persecutions, many Jews fled to France, where persecution was discouraged by powerful kings dependent on Jews for their skills in money management, medical treatment, and foreign diplomacy. (The Jews were highly literate, spoke multiple languages, and held the advantage of a decentralized intelligence network extending across the empire and beyond.) The Jews had learned to develop critical assets, such as a superior knowledge of medicine, astronomy, and the nature of money as a means of survival. By becoming the best doctors, and often saving the lives of family members of princes and aristocrats, the Jews made themselves all the more valuable and thereby tended to receive protection from the common rabble who were easily stirred to violence by the zealously anti-Jewish clergy.

As the political leadership of western and central Europe came increasingly under pressure from the rising power of the priesthood, the Jewish situation grew precarious. In the eleventh century it positively exploded.

By the end of the eleventh century, the Arab

Muslims had occupied Palestine for over four hundred years. A combination of factors led the Catholic Church to call for a European Crusade to capture the "Holy Land" from the "infidels." Traveling preachers journeyed through Europe stirring up support for the Crusade, and streamlining the motto, "God Wills It!" Christians were assured that anyone who died in the Crusade would be absolved of all sin and proceed directly to Paradise.

The movement reached a level of mob insanity in 1096, when a large ragtag army, consisting mostly of poor and illiterate peasants stirred to a frenzy by popular preachers, swept out of northern France and down through the German Rhineland. Their goal was to reach Palestine and take vengeance on the "infidels" (as the Muslims were called for the rejection of Jesus as the Christ). Upon reaching the German city of Cologne in April, with its significant Jewish population, it occurred to the Crusaders that the Jews were no less infidels than the Muslims. From city to city the Crusaders marched south along the Rhine River. Eight hundred Jews were massacred in Worms, one thousand in Mainz, and many others in Speyer, Cologne, and Trier. Reaching the Danube River, they turned east and slaughtered Jews in Regensberg, then on to Metz and Prague and throughout Bohemia. When Jerusalem was captured in July 1099, the Jews who could be found were herded into synagogues and burned alive.

Until the time of the First Crusade, the persecution of European Jews north of Spain had been episodic. Beginning in 1096, it became a continuum lasting four hundred years and culminating in the expulsions of the surviving Jews from England, France, Spain, southern Italy, and Sicily.

In 1144, a boy named William in Norwich, England, was found dead with several puncture wounds in his head. Word spread that Jews had killed him in a mock ceremony of the crucifixion of Jesus. No proof was ever offered, but dozens of Jews were hanged. From that time, the unsolved murders of children throughout Europe were blamed on local Jews, leading to incidents such as the 1171 burning of thirty-one Jewish men, women, and children in the French town of Blois. By the end of the century, Jewish people were routinely massacred for every imaginable reason, often on Sunday afternoons after fiery anti-Jewish sermons.

In England in 1189, the entire Jewish community of Lynn was slaughtered; the Jewish quarter in London was also burned and thirty Jews were killed. In 1190, five hundred were killed in York, fifty-seven in Bury St. Edmunds, and dozens more in Norwich. In the year 1217, the Jews of England were forced to wear badges. In 1278, the property of the wealthiest Jews throughout the country was confiscated, and three hundred were hanged. In 1290, the remaining sixteen thousand Jews in England were expelled and their property confiscated. Jews were not allowed to return to England for over 350 years, when a shift in sentiment was introduced by Oliver Cromwell and the ascendant Puritans.

In 1219, the Jews in France were forced to wear badges. In 1220, the badges were instituted in Sicily, and later also in the Papal States, then in Spain, Baghdad, Egypt, Germany, Austria, and Hungary. In 1267, the Jews in Poland and Austria were required to wear pointed hats. In Rome in 1360, they were forced to wear red capes, and in Barcelona in 1397, green costumes. In 1415 in Salzburg, pointed hats were required for the men, and bells on dresses for the women.

In 1191, one hundred Jews were burned alive in Paris. In 1218, in Neustadt on the border of Czechoslovakia, seventy-one were killed. In 1241, the entire Jewish community of 150 was killed in Frankfurt for attempting to persuade a Jew to refuse baptism. In Munich, 180 were burned alive in 1285. In 1288, 104 were killed in Bonn. In 1289, over 140 entire Jewish communities in central Europe were destroyed during the Rindfleisch massacres; 728 Jews were killed in Nuremberg alone.

The thirteenth century had been very bad, but the fourteenth century would be much worse. In southern France, 120 Jewish communities were destroyed in 1320; 500 Jews died in Verdun alone, and other 115 at Toulouse. The following year, 160 were killed in Chinon, and all Jewish property was confiscated. In 1328, six thousand were killed in eastern Spain. During the Armleder massacres of 1336–37, 110 Jewish communities in Germany and France were destroyed. From 1348–50, three hundred communities were destroyed in central and western Europe. In some cases, entire neighborhoods of Jews were annihilated. Six thousand died in Mainz, two thousand in Strasbourg, three thousand in Erfurt, twelve hundred in Salzburg, six hundred in Basle, five hundred in Brussels, four hundred in Worms, and three hundred fifty in Constance. Throughout Bavaria, twelve thousand were killed during those two years. In 1384, the entire community of Nordlingen was massacred. Thousands were killed in Prague in 1389 after a Jew threw a handful of dirt at a priest. In Spain (which was gradually being retaken by Catholic armies), four thousand were killed in Seville in 1391, four hundred in Barcelona, and thousands more during three months of rioting throughout Spain.

In 1394, the Jews were expelled from France as they had been from England.

The massacres continued into the fifteenth century. Seventy-seven were murdered in Prague in the year 1400. In Vienna, one hundred were burned in a field in 1421. In 1453, forty-one were burned in Breslau, with the rest expelled and their children confiscated to be raised in Christian homes. In Spain, there were mass murders in Cordoba in 1472, and even those who fled were hunted down and killed. In 1474, all the Jews of Segovia were murdered. In that same year, 860 were killed in Sicily. In 1486, twenty-four hundred died in Toledo.

In 1492, the Jews were expelled from Spain, where their ancestors had lived for over one thousand years. In that same year, they were also expelled from Sicily, and five years later from Portugal. In the 1497 expulsion from Portugal, Jewish children under age fourteen were confiscated and sent to Christian homes. At one point during the dramatic expulsion, hundreds of Jewish children were placed on ships to be taken to islands off the coast of Africa. Many of the parents drowned as they swam after the ships, pleading for the return of their children.

By the end of the century, no confessing Jews were left in western Europe. From England, through France, Spain, and Portugal, and around to Sicily and southern Italy, they had all been killed or expelled.

The expulsions intensified the Jewish experience of alienation in the world, and the longing for a return to their ancient homeland.

The Jews who fled from Spain settled mainly in Turkey, although many went north to the innovative city of Amsterdam, and others were scattered along the coast of North Africa. Some went to Galilee, where a movement that merged kabbalism and messianism developed and soon became the rage of eastern Jewry. This exhilarating mystical Judaism spread also to the northern European Jews who had fled from France and Germany into Poland, Lithuania, and the Ukraine.

It was in the far east of Europe that Jewish civilization now seemed to have found a stable place of sojourn. It was the best the Jews had experienced on such a broad scale since before the First Crusade, but it all came crashing down in the middle of the seventeenth century.

In 1648, a Ukrainian leader named Bohdan Chmielnicki led the Cossacks and the Polish peasantry in a violent campaign against the Jews. Over a period of about twelve months, more than one hundred thousand Jews were murdered. It was the worst Jewish massacre since the wars against Rome in the first and second centuries. It happened in a region to which they had fled from the horrific persecutions in central and western Europe. Hundreds of thousands now fled back toward the west, bringing astonishing reports of slaughter, rape, and mayhem that staggered the entire civilization of the Jews. "When Messiah comes, will there be any Jews left for the Return?" It was hardly a rhetorical question. The Jewish race/nation/religion (somewhere in that shifting complex of concepts is the actual description of what a Jewish person is), having held fast to the rabbinic model for a very long time, found itself pushed to the edge of its collective imagination. It seemed that, before too much longer, something would need to give. If Messiah did not come soon to lead the Jews back to Palestine—the land they had prayed for, dreamed of, and sent taxes to consistently for sixteen hundred years—perhaps they would need to reevaluate some of their standard assumptions.

Since their land had been taken and occupied by the Romans, the Jewish soul had sought internal refuge in an ever-developing system of self-interpretation, striving for a redeeming explanation of their sustained civilizational torment. Early generations of rabbis provided the generic framework. Israel was paying the penalty for its sins, and the suffering was a test of their resolve to cling faithfully to their God. The Exile was a necessary process on the way to Israel's ultimate purification and restoration in its ancient land. It must now be their duty and passion to pursue the Law, pray for the Restoration, and forward an annual tax (Halukkah) to the small and fledgling Jewish community that managed to endure the challenges of remaining in Palestine. (This annual tax never ceased to be observed by the Jews, so that even the poorest and most faraway communities sent a portion of their earnings as a way of contributing to the maintenance of a

Jewish presence in Palestine.)

By the third century, the explanation of the Exile had expanded to include the idea of a mission to the world. Along with working out its own purification, Israel was taking the knowledge of God to the nations. As their difficulties began escalating in the fourth and fifth centuries, the efforts to explain the Exile were intensified. Israel in its suffering was bearing not only its own sins, but also the sins of the nations. Israel was a priest to the world. The return to Jerusalem would not be realized until this mission was completed. The very fact that Jews were generally forbidden to own land was a good thing, as ownership of foreign land tended to inordinately attach them to the places of their sojourn, lessening the yearning for the Return.

In the tenth century, members of the Karaites, a splinter group of Middle Eastern Jews, began coming to Jerusalem on a mission of perpetual mourning. Calling themselves "The Mourners of Zion," they lived their entire lives in continual weeping and prayer for the Restoration of Israel in Palestine. In the years immediately following the First Crusade, the European Jewish scholar Rashi explained that since Jewish persecution among the nations was a confirmation of Israel's election, as a matter of metaphysical principle the Jews would not cease to be persecuted so long as the Exile continued. So long as they journeyed in foreign lands, the persecution would not end. This understanding of the situation compelled them to renew all the more their efforts to conform perfectly to the Law, thereby hastening the coming of Messiah and the regathering in Palestine.

The remarkable twelfth-century Jewish poet, Judah Halevi, explained that Israel is the heart of the human body, and that its suffering attests to its centrality in the plan of God. Jews should not only bear the Exile, but they should bear it *willingly*. In central and eastern Europe, the doctrine of *kiddush-ha-shem* developed, instructing Jews to show a stoical indifference when persecuted. This was a powerful psychological tool, placing the mind of the sufferer on a plateau that his or her tormentors could not reach by any means of oppression or torture. The great North African Jewish scholar Maimonides urged Israel in the twelfth century to hold fast to the end, exhorting them to understand that the persecutions of the Exile were another effort of Satan to turn Israel from its God.

The Spanish Jew Nachmanides, in the thirteenth century, developed a new concept in Israel's effort to understand the Exile. The physical suffering of Israel was the reflection of an invisible crisis. So long as Israel was removed from Palestine, the chief emanation of the essence of God Himself was in Exile. The struggle of the Jews was the outworking of a cosmic drama. This turn toward messianic and redemptive mysticism was developed from the doctrines of the Jewish *kabbalah* that first emerged in southern France in the twelfth century and flourished in Spain until the expulsion of 1492. (These doctrines quite obviously drew from the third-century teachings of the Gentile philosopher Plotinus.)

The leap into a mystical understanding of the Exile intensified among those who had left Spain, and in the sixteenth century it spread also among the Jewish communities of eastern Europe and the Ukraine. This was not an eclipse of the early rabbinic explanation, but rather a sophisticated development within the framework of that explanation. It gave to the Jews a dramatically expanded sense of the significance of their sufferings, and it served to energize their dream of returning to Palestine. During the seventeenth century, messianic-kabbalism, along with the ghastly slaughters in eastern Europe, fueled a Jewish mass movement centered in an apparent Messiah named Shabbetai Zevi. Even many of the rabbis in eastern Europe and throughout North Africa and the Ottoman Empire were swept into this movement centered on Zevi. The word among the Jews, far and wide, was that the Messiah had appeared and in the year 1666 would lead the Jews back to Palestine. The movement crashed when Zevi was arrested by Turkish authorities and converted to Islam to save his life.

Combined with the Chmielnicki massacres, the crushing disappointment of Zevi prepared Jewish civilization for radically new conceptual experiments. In the middle of the eighteenth century, a Jewish mystic in Poland, later called the Baal Shem Tov by his followers, headed a movement that shattered the monopoly of the rabbis over Jewish thought and life. This was the Hasidic movement, focusing on prayer and communion and the joyous celebration of being a Jew. The Hasidic movement of eastern Europe coincided approximately with a very different Jewish movement in north-central Europe, primarily in Berlin and Paris.

The European Enlightenment was promoting among the Gentiles a comprehensive secularizing process in which, among other things, new philosophies of self-identity were eclipsing the traditional religious explanations of human value and purpose. Rather than thinking of themselves primarily or even necessarily as *Christians,* the intellectuals of Europe began viewing themselves as "human beings" who may or may not happen to be Christians. (This was, of course, a very generic concept that would later be filled with particular and often destructive content.) This direction of thought was captured in the remark of a Jew following the burning of an eighteen-year-old Jewish girl in Lisbon by the Inquisitors. The remark was quoted approvingly by Montesquieu, a leading French representative of the Enlightenment: "You want us [the Jews] to be Christians, but you yourselves do not want to be Christians. But if you do want to be Christians, at least be human beings" (quoted from Hans Kung, *Judaism,* The Crossroad Publishing Company, 1992, p. 196).

The idea of the Enlightenment was that all men, regardless of race, religion, or nationality, should recognize certain basic human values. Since all human beings are intrinsically equal, and the Jews are human beings, there is no logical justification for denying a Jew the full rights of citizenship and all that goes with it. "Tolerance" and "freedom" became key words. Many of the leading Jews in France and Germany were fascinated with this concept, and began insisting the Jewish Exile need not wait for a return to Palestine for its termination. The Exile could end right where they were. The dominant Jewish intellectual of the eighteenth century, Moses Mendelssohn, argued that to be "Jewish" was strictly a private religious affair and should not be understood in terms of "nationality." Jews living in Germany, he insisted, should be considered no less *German* than the Gentiles living in Germany. German Jews who followed the lead of Mendelssohn began referring to themselves as "Germans of the Mosaic religion," and to their Gentile neighbors as "Germans of the Christian religion." Rather than maintaining the cultural *separation* enforced by the rabbinic model, the "enlightened Jews" believed *assimilation* was a more proper pursuit for the Jewish people.

So in Germany and France they danced with Gentiles, for a time. It seemed a very happy marriage. The movement spread east as far as Russia, where Jewish intellectuals articulated a vision incompatible with the separatist model of the rabbis. The "enlightened" Russian Jews began collaborating with the Czarist government for the implementation of programs designed to reduce rabbinic influence and integrate the millions of Russian Jews into the cultural mainstream. This vision came crashing down with the anti-Jewish riots that exploded across western Russia after the assassination of Czar Alexander II.

Although the philosophy of the Enlightenment saw no *logical justification* for denying equality, fraternity, and the full advantages of citizenship to the Jews, human beings tend to be guided by sentiment far more so than by a regard for logical consistency. For all of the titillating highbrow philosophy, the fact remained that European and Russian Gentiles had inherited a deeply passionate hatred and fear of the Jews (who for centuries had been consistently caricatured as the Christ-killers, the child-murderers, the money-sucking loan sharks and the capitalists). The Czar's assassination created a temporary sense of anarchy that stripped the thinly veiled inhibitions of the Russian populace, and a series of horrific anti-Jewish riots (pogroms) broke out first in the Ukraine, then spread east toward Moscow and west through Poland and Lithuania. From 1881–84, tens of thousands of Jews were killed, and nearly two million fled westward into central Europe. The dream of the eastern assimilationists was crushed, and in the Polish city of Warsaw a *Jewish nationalist movement was founded.* For eighteen centuries they had waited for the Messiah, and things had only gotten worse. Perhaps Messiah, after all, was in the barrel of a gun! The essence of Zionism is a secularization and militarization of the Messiah doctrine. It is not merely a reaction to persecution and discrimination, but also a passionate affirmation of Jewish self-consciousness and self-determination in modern, non-religious terms.

If the French could shake off a religiously informed self-identity, and take militant pride in their ancestry and homeland (which was the next step in the secularizing Enlightenment process), and if the Germans, Poles, Russians, Swiss, and Serbs could do the same, why should the Jews not also assume an aggressive pride in their nation and their homeland? For centuries they had looked to ancient pious scholars for inspiration. Perhaps now it was time to look to Samson and Judas Maccabee.

It was a long and tortured road from the rabbis of Galilee to the Zionists of Europe. But on one point the rabbis and the Zionists unequivocally agreed: Palestine is the authentic geographical and spiritual homeland of the Jewish people.

While the assimilationist dream had died in the east, the Jews in the west of Europe were still enjoying their cultural dance with the Gentiles, remaining committed to the first-phase Enlightenment vision. This vision died when the fully assimilated French-Jewish Colonel Alfred Dreyfus was charged with treason (it was later proven that Dreyfus was framed). The streets of Paris became a shocking orgy of anti-Jewish demonstrations. This was not an expression of traditional, religiously inspired contempt and suspicion toward the Jews, but rather of the modern, racially motivated form of *anti-Semitism*. Although the French authorities permitted no violence, the message was driven home to the European Jewish assimilationists. Theodore Herzl, a fully assimilated Viennese journalist on assignment in Paris, understood that message and concluded that the only remaining hope for Jewish civilization was the reconstitution of a Jewish state in a national homeland. In 1897, Herzl presided as president over the First Zionist Congress in Basle, Switzerland. Eighteen centuries of momentum had accumulated, and the Return was now an idea knocking at the door.

The history of the Zionist movement is one of the more fascinating subjects of study in all of world history. It is a tremendous confluence of energies, philosophies, and talented personalities striving to capture a new threshold. It is also a superlative lesson in the values of commitment, self-determination, and ruthless optimism shouting down the voices of naysayers and crushing the doubts within their own minds. Zionism is a concretization of multiple universal human archetypes, some good and some evil, but all inviolable in the kind of world we are consigned to. The Zionist parallels with the historical psychology of America are profound, as we have enormous respect for a self-made country that started from scratch against unspeakable odds in an oppressive world. The Zionists, like the Americans, are a people who "get it done" because it must get done, and it was a Jew (Hillel) who challenged us all with the searing questions: "If not us, who? If not now, when?"

The Zionists, like the Americans, have answered these questions unequivocally in their every moment of truth. Although our system is not isomorphically workable in Israel's situation, they have developed a stable form of democracy commensurate with real-world possibilities.

The Return began as a trickle. By the year 1900, fifty thousand Jews were in Palestine (up from about twenty-five thousand fifty years earlier). By 1914, there were eighty-five thousand. From 1917–21, a shocking series of pogroms again broke out in Russia, with up to one hundred thousand Jews massacred, leading to a new wave of immigration. In the following decade, the rise of fascism in central Europe, and most emphatically the swearing in of the Nazi Party in 1933, led to another wave of immigrants. By 1939, the official beginning of World War II, there were over four hundred thousand Jews in Palestine. The Arabs who had occupied Palestine since the seventh century were resistant, but the Jews had nowhere left to go and, furthermore, believed their claim on the land was prior to the claims of any other surviving people. David Ben Gurion explained after a series of violent Arab riots in late 1936:

> We are here in our own right. We regard the Jewish National Home as an end in itself. We claim to be here and to assure our future here because it is our own right and it is justified in itself. . .
>
> Our right in Palestine is not derived from the [decisions of the United Nations and the British government]. It is prior to that. . . Our right [to

have a Jewish state in Palestine] is as old as the
Jewish people. . . It is because we are the children of the Jewish people and it is the only homeland of the Jewish people that we have rights in
this country. . .

We came to create. . . Our aim is to make
the Jewish people master of its own destiny, not
subject to the will and mercy of others, as any
other free people. (*The Jew in the Modern World*,
edited by Paul Mendes-Flohr and Jehuda
Reinharz, Oxford University Press, 1995, pp.
604–5)

Are the Zionists "right" in this? Is that question relevant in a time of war? Would an answer to that question
make any difference in what the outcome of events will be?

World War II was decisive in the next phase of the
Zionist movement. The Holocaust was by far the most sen-
sational display of human evil in the history of the world.
The leader of the Palestinian Arabs, Amin al-Husseini, lived
as an honored guest in Berlin from 1941–45. He was broad-
casting Nazi propaganda, organizing the recruitment of
Arab Muslims to fight alongside the Nazis, and working
with the Nazi High Command in the development of a
blueprint for expanding the Final Solution to Palestine and
the entire Middle East in case the Nazis should win the war.

We do well to keep in mind that these things did not
occur in a long-ago period. Many people are alive today who
participated in these crimes, and many are alive who survived as victims. In the Central European Holocaust, the
capacities of an advanced industrial superpower were har-
nessed and coordinated for the purpose of completing what
the Crusaders had begun. So much Jewish flesh was burned
in Europe that the air we breathe today is buzzing with the
molecules of the bodies of the millions of men, women, and

children slaughtered by the Nazis and their sympathizers. Prior to the Second World War, the Jewish nationalists struggled for support. But Zionism was galvanized in the nightmare of the Holocaust. Chaim Potok has somewhere written of a comment he heard as a youth from an older relative: "There are no more gentle Jews. Even the Hasidim are no longer gentle."

After the death of Bar Kochba in 135, there were no more Samsons, only pious scholars. Samson was resurrected in the death camps of Central Europe, and now the world must contend with him. The leader of the Palestinians sided with the Nazis and advocated an expansion of the death camp system, but the force of history emerging from that system is now vastly more powerful than those who seek to oppose it.

On May 14, 1948, David Ben Gurion announced from Tel Aviv the reconstitution of the *State of Israel* in Palestine. The government of the United States of America immediately announced to the world that it recognized the State of Israel, and that it would establish full diplomatic relations with the government of that state. The governments of the surrounding Arab nations announced to the world that they did *not* recognize the State of Israel, and that it had no right to exist in Palestine (this is still the effective position of the Arab League). Twelve hours after Ben Gurion's announcement, five Arab nations invaded Palestine with the declared aim of "driving Israel into the Sea." We know the story.

In the land of Palestine today, two thousand years of momentum are crashing against thirteen hundred years of inertia. The outcome is already certified, although the form it will take is not yet clear.

What is clear is that America has a civilizational investment in Israel, and that the Palestinian community is dominated and represented by terrorists who hate Americans just as they hate Israelis. While the Israelis wept *with us* on September 11, the Palestinians danced in the streets.

An article in the October 6 issue of *The Economist* highlighted a relevant point: "If the Jewish state did not exist, America's relations with the Arabs would be simpler. James Forrestal, America's defense secretary, foresaw this in 1948, when he tried to talk Harry Truman out of recognizing the new state, lest this antagonized the Arabs and hampered American access to their oil. But since Israel does exist, and has a birth certificate from the United Nations, it is right for America to support it."

Although I personally care little for "a birth certificate from the United Nations," I care very much for the investment our nation has made in the success of Israel.

If we are actually thinking to "rid the world of evil," we might first look to our own backyard (including the presidential papers of a previous administration). We have plenty of unattended issues at home. But if we can set aside the hubris about a war of good against evil (which restricts our options to what helps us morally flatter ourselves) and concentrate with less pietistic extravagance upon the need to *swiftly* liquidate the enemy trying to kill us (not merely in Afghanistan, but worldwide), we will not only consider invoking our ultimate capacity, but we will also stand shoulder to shoulder with the friend and ally who is fighting this war on the front lines with its back to the wall.

13.   The World Has Grown Too Small for Tolerating What We Could Once Safely Allow

Our ability to be a free and open society in an age of knowledge and mass travel depends on a willingness to use our prerogative of power in the face of any threat.

Our world of nations has become an orgy of penetration. The seventeenth-century concept of nations as billiard balls on a table is fundamentally inapplicable in the twenty-first century. The world has become too small, too intertwined, and too dangerous for a continued toleration of some of our long-held geopolitical assumptions.

Since the world is no longer so sharply divided by nations, but is rather an entanglement of nations, whatever is allowed in one territory will, sooner rather than later, project its momentum among the others.

The threat to us can no longer be contained. Since this became shockingly evident on September 11, we must acclimate our sensibilities to the newly dominant geopolitical reality: What cannot be contained must be removed.

Our civilizational model is based on a handful of powerful ideas, all working in tandem. Three of these dominant ideas are freedom, progress, and equality. If we truly believe in our model of liberal democracy, we will want all human beings to enjoy the integrity of freedom and self-determination. Freedom, that is, to make their own choices within a consistently formulated legal framework, with the lawmakers themselves elected to limited terms by the free and equal votes of the citizenry.

If we truly believe democracy is the most humane and productive form of government, and if organized opposition to our model now represents a lethal threat to our security, then our most humane and survivalist impulses will instruct us of the need to eliminate that opposition.

Our doctrine of freedom is not what the citizens of

the frustrated Muslim nations despise. What disturbs them is how America uses one hand to provide freedom for its own people, while using the other to support governments that brutally forbid freedom. The Saudi royal family is, after the Taliban, among the most brutally repressive regimes on the planet. The commoners of Saudi Arabia are hardly citizens according to our understanding of the word. The range of freedoms allowed them under the Saudi regime is revoltingly narrow (particularly for the women), and even the hint of desire for greater freedom is answered with horrifically severe punishments. So the irony of the situation is that the terrorist-supporting (or at least sympathizing) citizens of those nations are naturally attracted to the concept of freedom, but the governments that prevent them from reaching for this freedom are able to retain their power largely by the support of the government of the United States. These hundreds of millions of oppressed and exploited Muslims have quite naturally become a massive pool of potential recruits for Islamic terrorists. After we have destroyed the Islamic militant movement, we should act to remove the terror of governments that oppose freedom.

The only way of "making the world safe for democracy" is to comprehensively dismantle (by whatever means) organized resistances to democracy, whether it be the terrorists or the freedom-suppressing governments.

The terrorists recognize it is no longer possible for any large cultural grouping to successfully resist the Euro-American consensus. They very well understand that distance and borders are no longer effective buffers against the encroachments of alternative concepts of life. Since their perverse ideas of God and of human nature disallow their cooperation with our model of freedom, progress, and equality, they have launched a violent struggle that will only end with the extinction of either their way of life or ours. They understand the present day far better than the anti-war demonstrators in America and Europe do. The age we have entered is swiftly imploding the possibility of coexistence between radically conflicting socio-economic models on this planet. This is not a grandiose idea, but a simple acknowledgment of the direction of history and the limited structural possibilities of a shrinking world.

In the final analysis, we seem to have only two choices: the global investment of our consensus (by force if necessary) or anarchy (abroad and, eventually, at home). Since the earth, in many respects, is becoming a "global village," we no longer have the luxury of tolerating armed and organized commitments to a model or anti-model that cannot coexist with our own system. We have reached an age in which it is either our way or theirs.

We were able to safely tolerate such a coexistence only so long as those who opposed us did not attempt to destroy us. The assault upon our homeland with weapons of mass destruction has obliterated for us the luxury of toleration. We must impose our model, or eventually our model will be ripped to shreds. Our civilization, due to the nature of an open society in an age of dangerous knowledge and mass travel, no longer has the luxury of safely accommodating opposing models or anti-models. The world has simply gotten too small.

This would not be arrogance on our part, but rather the straightforward recognition of a genuine imperative created by a new age. No one disputes that we cannot allow armed and organized opposition to our way of life within our own borders. We can allow protests and demonstrations against specific policies or decisions, but not an armed and organized resistance to the American democracy. To allow such a thing within our borders would threaten the fundamental security of our nation. On September 11, we were stunningly confronted with the reality that we have already entered a new epoch. In this epoch, the world of nations is so small and intertwined that we can no longer safely tolerate armed and organized resistance to democracy outside of our borders. To allow it outside of our country is to invite it into our country.

If we are not willing to boldly, carefully, and comprehensively exercise our capacity to streamline democracy among the web of nations, can America and its true allies actually remain free and open societies?

In this new epoch, I do not believe we can long remain open and free without the aggressive kneading of our civilizational investments—our investments of freedom and of progress and of equality—among the global continuum. It seems that only by this means can we continue offering the advantages of our nation and its system to those from other parts of the world.

Some theoreticians tell us that democracy is incompatible with many cultures in the world. The facts of history call this thesis into question. If Taiwan has become a flourishing democracy, Mainland China has the indomitable impulse to become one also. If South Koreans have emerged as lovers of freedom, why should we suppose their kin in the north would not display the same impulse if given the chance? If the land of the Sultans proved compatible with freedom, so can the land of the Sheiks. If the children of Hirohito have embraced the consensus, we have no reason for denying the knowledge that freedom—as we have come to understand it and to express it in terms of political democracy and free-market economics—is an instinctive craving in the deepest mind of every sane human being. As Fukuyama has compellingly argued, history itself testifies that the love of freedom is a universal constant.

Another outstanding testimony to the universal appeal of freedom is the empirical fact that from every nation and every culture they *come to America.* Why do they come here? Why is it that masses of Americans do not migrate *there?*

They come to the freedom symbolized in the Statue of Liberty, despised by all who despise the freedom of everyone but themselves.

The world has become too small for the Statue in New York Harbor and for those who want to destroy it.

In the swiftly evolving global village, where a sneeze in Indonesia sends germs into America, uncooperative cultural groupings cannot be tolerated if they present a threat to the security and prosperity of those who belong to the dominant consensus. This consensus holds than an individual's right to the pursuit of freedom, progress, and equality is conferred by birth, and from birth it is inalienable.

This doctrine is an honest and self-consistent acknowledgment of the imperatives imposed upon us by a new epoch, and by the violence of those who oppose us in the contest for survival within this epoch. In this confrontation with the opponents of freedom, we should act in a manner that will reconcile their understandings to the realities of power and to the direction of history in the twenty-first century. It is a century requiring extreme solutions and extreme readjustments in the way the world is organized. History is on our side, but if we fail to read the time and seize the hour we will have lost the favor of history.

Pursuing this achievable goal of universal democracy would bring us into an existential symbiosis with the momentum of history and with the universal love of freedom. It would also give us the satisfaction of imputing a supreme historical irony to the memory of Osama bin Laden and the movement he had symbolized.

Part Four:

Justification for the Debate

14.   An Attack Justifies a Response

In principle, does a catastrophic *attack* with weapons of mass destruction not justify a debate on the terms and conditions that would legitimate a *response* with our most formidable weapons?

In terms of principle, there could be no greater justification than this.

On what grounds can it be denied that our enemies themselves have provided us with a principled justification *if* we were to choose to invoke our ultimate capacity? The use of hijacked commercial airliners as guided missiles, with a destruction capacity of such magnitude that a single strike could demolish a 100–story tower, certainly qualifies as an unconventional weapon of mass destruction.

There *may* be other considerations that would compel us to impose such a restraint upon ourselves, but in principle our enemies themselves have already justified for us the option of debating the role of our ultimate weapons in this current, lethal crisis. Whatever the *outcome* of the debate, there is no logical reason for Americans to feel unethical about the debate itself.

15. Our Ideology Exists for Us, Not We for It

"For too long . . . we have ignored Islamic clarion calls for our destruction" (William J. Bennett).

In 1998, Osama bin Laden issued a statement to Muslims worldwide, insisting it is their religious duty to kill Americans *wherever they can be found*. Since then, bin Laden's organization, which also functions as a compass and a symbol of focus for Islamic terrorist groups in dozens of countries, has murdered *thousands* of Americans in increasingly audacious suicide attacks. The most notable of these are the 1998 suicide bombings of U.S. embassies in Kenya and Tanzania, which slaughtered hundreds; the 2000 suicide bombing of the *USS Cole* in the Persian Gulf, which killed seventeen of our unsuspecting sailors; and the recent suicide attacks on the East Coast of the United States.

Since September 11, al Qaeda and its associates have escalated their threats against American civilization. On October 9, a widely viewed Arab television news station (Al Jazeera, which is a principal news source and voice of influence for tens of millions of Middle Eastern Muslims) aired a video message from al Qaeda spokesman Sulaiman abu Ghaith, which included the following excerpts (as quoted in the October 10 issue of the *Los Angeles Times*): "These youths who did what they did and destroyed America with their airplanes, they've done a good deed. They have moved the battle into the heart of America. . . The Americans must know that the storm of airplanes will not stop, and there are thousands of young people who look forward to death like the Americans look forward to living. . . We shall be victorious: The Americans have opened a door that will never be closed."

In this statement, abu Ghaith is effectively boasting of al Qaeda's role in the September 11 massacres. He is also vowing the terrorist assault on America will not only continue, but that it will escalate.

The *Times* article (by senior staff writer Robin Wright) further reported: "Abu Ghaith also called on Muslims in more than 50 nations to 'uphold their religion' by attacking American interests worldwide. . . . Abu Ghaith warned that the new war against the United States will target all American facilities and personnel. . . . [Abu Ghaith decreed that] 'jihad today is a duty of every Muslim. . . God says fight. . . The American interests are everywhere, all over the world. Every Muslim has to play his real and true role to uphold his religion. And fighting and jihad are a duty.'"

For the past several years, Islamic terrorist organizations have consistently pledged to kill Americans wherever they can be found. Just two weeks before the September 11 attacks, a columnist for a government-sponsored Egyptian daily newspaper wrote: "The Statue of Liberty, in New York Harbor, must be destroyed. . . The age of the American collapse has begun."

This call to arms was issued in the Egyptian national press. If I were to catalogue even a small percentage of such *documented terrorist threats* against America in recent years, I would need an entire shelf on which to stack the paper. William J. Bennett wrote in the October 1 issue of the *Los Angeles Times:* "For too long we . . . have ignored Islamic clarion calls for our destruction."

Sworn testimony has been given that the al Qaeda terrorist camps in Afghanistan provided sophisticated training in the use of chemical and biological agents. Sworn testimony has also been given that an al Qaeda operative had arranged for the purchase of a canister of uranium, although the former terrorist who provided the testimony was uncertain whether or not the transaction had actually been completed. If so, this would mean bin Laden and his associates have enough radioactive material to inflict an excruciating death on tens of thousands of Americans. Do they plan to use these instruments of death in their campaign to destroy us? Is it *reasonable* for us to give such enemies "the benefit of the doubt" on any issue of lethal consequence?

A critical value in the ideology that regulates our civilization is summarized in the maxim "Innocent until *proven* guilty." This is a powerful judicial concept, and its domestic application to all U.S. citizens is indispensable to our way of life. Yet what do we do when the implementation of our ideology strains the security of our civilization to the breaking point?

We do not know who is directly responsible for the anthrax mail attacks, but we do know that thousands of Islamic militants have trained for such assaults, and they have threatened to use chemical, biological, and nuclear weapons against American civilians. The logic of realpolitik reminds us that our ideology exists for us, not we for it. Will we become slaves of what ought to serve us? If our ideology is serving our enemies more effectively than it is serving us, we have been hamstrung by idealism and we are no longer being faithful to our national philosophy.

The outcome of the Cold War is our most recent historical example of the ever-present need to approach the world on various, simultaneous levels of evaluation. Our success in the Cold War was forged in a complementarity of ideology and realpolitik.

There is no contradiction between these spheres of logic. If we do not permit the one to condition our implementation of the other, the final triumph of our ideology will be its triumph against us in the twisted hands of our enemies.

The most forceful articulation of the widespread Islamic vow to destroy American civilization has come directly from the mouth of bin Laden. The following is from the infamous text of his taped remarks released to an Arab television station on October 8 (the day after the U.S. commenced its bombing campaign in Afghanistan): "There is America, hit by God in one of its softest spots. Its greatest buildings were destroyed, thank God for that. There is America, full of fear from its north to its south, from its west to its east. Thank God for that. . . God has blessed a group of vanguard Muslims, the forefront of Islam, to destroy America. May God bless them and allot them a supreme place in heaven. . . These events have divided the whole world into two sides. The side of believers and the side of infidels. . . Every Muslim has to rush to make his religion victorious. . . To America, I say only a few words to it and its people: I swear to God that America will not live in peace" (quoted from the October 8 issue of the *Los Angeles Times*).

These are words from a man already responsible for the slaughter of thousands of Americans. We ourselves have not chosen the need to debate the conditions under which an ultimate response would be, all things considered, in line with both our values and our security imperatives. Our enemies have chosen this need for us.

It is possible that al Qaeda is not directly responsible for the spread of anthrax through the U.S. mail system, and that it is not planning attacks of such a nature against America. Yet if we know they have trained their men in the deadly arts of chemical and biological warfare, have pledged the name and the power of their god to the death of our civilization, and have already murdered thousands of our people and are promising to do much more, do we have the luxury of declaring them "innocent until proven guilty"?

Do we gamble the security of our nation, with the potential loss of millions of American lives, on "the benefit of a doubt" against indiscriminate murderers committed to our destruction? With regard to the anthrax, do we truly have the luxury of declaring Saddam Hussein "innocent until proven guilty"? If we wait too long for proof, we will likely have waited too long.

How much do we tolerate before initiating a serious discussion on the terms and conditions under which the use of our ultimate weapons would be consistent with our most fundamental values and imperatives? If such a measure could promise a swift triumph at the psychological level, perhaps it is our moral obligation, if not to ourselves then at least to our children, to debate such a measure.

If al Qaeda is not directly responsible for the current attacks with deadly bacteria, their use of hijacked airplanes as guided missiles in the most populated region of our country is the impact equivalent of an attack with unconventional weapons of mass destruction. On every conceivable ground, we as a nation are justified in launching a vigorous public debate on the potential use of our ultimate weapons to achieve the psychological triumph that would destroy the worldwide momentum of the terrorist mass movement. Perhaps an intense public debate, merely in itself, would strengthen our government's hand as it negotiates with the world on issues of unprecedented scale.

Part Five:

Homeland Issues

16.   The Constitution and Collective Rights

A decisive material and psychological triumph over al Qaeda would not cancel or mitigate the need to enhance our homeland security system.

There is an old argument claiming "it is better for one hundred guilty to go free than for one innocent to be convicted." This argument grows porous under a more consistent analysis. Of the one hundred guilty who go free, over half will commit new crimes, creating fifty innocent victims to complement the one hundred previous victims who found no justice under the judicial logic of "better one hundred than one."

We cannot eat our cake and still have it. When generosity is made a principle rather than a contingency, leeches gather to this principle and suck the blood of the generous. When John Ashcroft was summoned before the Senate in early December to answer Congressional concerns about the legal rights of accused terrorists, the Attorney General began by holding up a copy of the al Qaeda training manual. The *Wall Street Journal* explained in its December 7 "Review & Outlook" section: "[The al Qaeda training manual] describes how terrorists have been instructed to use America's civil-rights protections to their own destructive advantage."

In carrying our generosity to such an extreme, we enabled our enemies to borrow a chapter from Homer and to spill their destruction across our land on a sleepy summer morning. A difference between us and the unsuspecting Trojans is that Western governments received loud and consistent warnings that a nest of enemies had been setting up deadly operations in our midst from the hidden belly of a civilized Islamic community. We can be reasonably certain the nineteen hijackers were not the only al Qaeda members to have entered the U.S. and to have set in motion a carefully developed series of plans for horrific destruction against America. Our government, by means of bold and aggressive crime-fighting tactics, has so far prevented (as of late December) any further terrorist activity by al Qaeda operatives within America.

The Bush administration, and particularly Attorney General John Ashcroft, has been loudly criticized by the press (in general) and by many in Congress for these aggressive tactics. A majority of Americans, however, support these measures in the context of the present crisis. V. S. Naipaul, author and Nobel Prize winner, has warned for years that the imbalanced Western emphasis on individual legal rights and humanitarianism is being exploited by a calculating enemy that finds ready cover for itself in a peaceful and law-abiding Islamic community. Jim Hoagland reports in the October 22 issue of the *Post Weekly:* "[Naipaul has] frequently warned that the West was living in 'false security' by failing to recognize and react against the imperial and aggressive nature of a vengeful cultural fanaticism cloaked in Islamic garb. 'They mistake the kindness and openness of America and Britain for weakness and will exploit it,' he told me some time ago. Today Naipaul finds no pleasure or particular merit in having been proved right."

Ralph Peters has bluntly observed: "The humanitarianism we cherish is regarded as a sign of impotence by such opponents . . . you cannot appease them any more than you could a Hitler" (*Post Weekly,* October 1).

This exploitation of Western naïveté has turned British soil into one of the world's most flourishing colonies of known international terrorists. Among the more outstanding examples of Britain's role, by default, in the nurturing of the Islamic terrorist movement is the case of Yasser Serri, an Egyptian terrorist mastermind living comfortably in London since 1994. The *Los Angeles Times* reported in its October 31 issue: "Yasser Serri, 38, whose Islamic Observation

Center serves as a propaganda arm of Islamic fundamental-ist groups, was also accused of soliciting support for a banned Egyptian extremist organization, Gamaa al Islamiya, fund-raising for a terrorist group and publishing material intended to incite racial hatred. . . Serri, in exile in Britain since 1994, has been sentenced to death in absentia in Egypt for an assassination attempt on the prime minister. The Egyptian government has been pressing Britain for his arrest and extradition for years."

Serri was the leader of a terrorist cell that tried to assassinate the Egyptian head of state. People were killed in that attempt. Egypt quite naturally wants this dangerous terrorist leader brought to justice. The British government has refused to hand Serri over to Egyptian authorities, claiming it is not their custom to expel a guest who would likely be executed by the government that seeks him. During the years in which our British friends have graciously hosted Serri and scores of his colleagues, Britain has not only served as a convenient base for the preparation of terrorist attacks against American interests, but also as a successful forum for a massive program of indoctrination among the British Islamic community. "Some polls say four out of ten British Muslims think al Qaeda's attacks are in some way justified; a handful have actually volunteered to fight with the Taliban" (*The Economist,* November 10).

The British homeland is in trouble for as far as the eye can see. Enhanced, common-sense anti-terrorist legisla-tion now is a dramatically needed security improvement, yet it will be a closing of the barn door after the horses are already out.

London, perhaps even more so than the popular Islamic terrorist resorts of Paris, Hamburg, and Milan, has become a key breeding ground for the terrorist mass move-ment. Zacarias Moussaoui, who is suspected of having been the original pilot-designee for Flight 93 (the Pennsylvania crash), received his indoctrination in London. In a stirring article on the front page of the December 13 issue of the *Los Angeles Times,* the grief and frustration of Moussaoui's mother is documented: "It pained her, she said, that she had lost [her son] to London, where police say he was a devoted follower of Amar Abu Qatada, who Spanish authorities say is Al Qaeda's chief European organizer. It was also in London, police say, that Zacarias Moussaoui grew close to two French converts to Islam who trained in Afghan camps. One of them has been arrested on suspicion of plotting to bomb the U.S. Embassy in Paris. . . She said she blamed 'those false imams in England who brainwashed my son and allowed all this to happen.'"

While I have no sympathy for Moussaoui—who, while seated in a dayroom watching television in an Arizona jail on September 11, leapt from his chair and shouted with approval when he first saw the filming of the mayhem in New York City—I have a deep regard for the grief of his mother. I also experience frustration over what I view as an obscene permissiveness on the part of our good friends in Britain. That great nation and staunch ally of the United States could stand to reassess some of its assumptions about the nature of toleration and the conditions under which it is feasible and not.

The December 17 issue of *Newsweek* reported on the contents of a Britain-based website, Assam Publications: "[The Islamist website] features virulent condemnations of the United States, includes links to recruitment pitches for 'martyrs.' . . . Investigators say the site is operated by Osama bin Laden supporters in Britain." This permissiveness is widespread throughout the Continent also: "Despite recent arrests across Europe, much remains to be done in the West to rein in terrorists. 'We believe 60% of radical Islamic networks are yet to be discovered here,' a Western European intelligence official said" (*Los Angeles Times,* December 9).

The running amok of terrorist recruitment, indoctrination, and organizational programs throughout Europe, under cover of the broader Islamic and Arab-immigrant community, is a natural consequence of the distorted European emphasis on humanitarian generosity and individual rights (at the expense of collective rights). Generosity is *not* respected by the criminal mind. It is assessed by the criminal mind as an exposure of weakness and gullibility, and its only appealing value to such a mind is the ease with which it can be exploited. We should recall the boasts of the Libyan immigrant, enjoying the rich advantages of civil rights and other benefits unavailable in his home country: "God loves us because Europe is in our hands . . . we are fighting-immigrants. This is our duty that we have to carry on with honor. . . We have to be like snakes. We have to strike and then hide."

The *Wall Street Journal* was impressively bold in raising a highly sensitive issue in its "Review & Outlook" section of December 14: "Americans also consider the death penalty to be a moral issue; some of us would call it a test of a civilization's seriousness in coping with the evil side of human nature revealed by the WTC mass murders. We'd even add that the French announcement of aid to Moussaoui is an example of the immoral appeasement that has allowed terrorists to run wild for 20 years. . . To adapt the Bush Doctrine to Europe, on bringing terrorists to justice, you're either for us or against us."

The Spanish government recently announced the arrests of eight members of al Qaeda, some of whom may have had a role in the September 11 attacks. The Spanish government has made it clear that it will not hand these terrorists over to America if doing so would subject them to the death penalty or to a military tribunal. One of the prominent reasons for the choice of the terrorist leaders to establish colonies in western Europe is their understanding that they will not be extradited for sponsoring terrorist activity, even if that activity is on the scale of what America suffered on September 11. We might ask our friends in Europe to consider the multitudes of innocent people murdered in terrorist schemes sponsored and planned in Europe. We are not asking them to implement a death penalty of their own, but to somehow adjust their policy so as to revoke this tactical advantage that they have handed to the terrorist movement.

In late September, the British arrested an Algerian named Lotfi Raissi, believed to be the lead instructor of the four pilots who steered the hijacked jets on September 11. The *Wall Street Journal* reported in its October 1 issue: "It could take up to three years for the U.S. to extradite [Raissi] from Britain . . . illustrating how drawn-out the war on terrorism may be. . . Besides Mr. Raissi, Britain currently is holding eight other alleged terrorists wanted by several countries—four by the U.S.—and some have been in jail fighting extradition for as long as three years. . . If ultimately the courts do rule in favor of extradition, Britain would hand Raissi over on a murder charge only if the U.S. gave a written guarantee that it wouldn't impose the death penalty. The deal in any extradition would obviously hamper efforts by U.S. prosecutors to win convictions against alleged conspirators in the Sept. 11 attacks."

I am curious as to what the response of our good friend Tony Blair might have been had the Taliban, back in September, offered to hand over bin Laden "only if the U.S. gave a written guarantee that it wouldn't impose the death penalty"?

This European emphasis on "rights" oddly leaves out the right of people to enjoy a *security* provided by their government. The *right of collective security* has been largely eclipsed by a distorted emphasis on the freedoms and protections of an individual in societies that have elevated generosity from a healthy contingency to an easily exploited principle.

America, of course, is not without its own challenges. A *Los Angeles Times* editorial on October 27
reported a disturbing situation in Washington, D.C.:

> Some junior high students at an Islamic reli-
> gious school in Washington, D.C., recently said
> that being an American means nothing more than
> being born here and that they don't believe
> Osama bin Laden is such a bad guy—views the
> school reportedly had encouraged. That even a
> few young people in today's melting pot hold
> such shocking notions [in truth, there are more
> than "a few"], and feel no particular allegiance to
> the nation that lets them freely express those
> views, should spur others to rethink what it
> means to live in this country. . .
>
> Every generation must discover for itself
> the responsibilities of citizenship, just as those
> who pulled the country through the extreme tests
> of national character did during three previous
> centuries. . .
>
> Schools that fail to inculcate a sense of com-
> mitment to this country do students a potentially
> crippling disservice.

The resolution of contradictions is an ongoing
imperative in the triumph of democracy. In view of the less
admirable tendencies of human nature, I believe the Western
system of liberal democracy is the best possible form of
social organization in an imperfect world. The situation will
always be dynamic, as the very nature of competing interests will prevent a stable center from ever actually emerging.
Sometimes, as a society, we find ourselves too far in one
direction (as with the internments of the 1940s), or too far in

another (as, perhaps, with the current reach of multicultural-ism). The genius of our system is such that we are com-pelled, from one generation to the next, to strive toward that unclear center in which our competing interests will cohabit in a stable equilibrium. As to what that center actually looks like, we do not know. But we are certain it cannot be approached without a due regard for freedom *and* equality, self-determination *and* social responsibility, individual rights *and* collective coherence. These are the values that simultaneously pull us away from equilibrium and toward it, so that the nature of our democracy involves the restless pur-suit of what we will never fully possess.

When a series of powerful contradictions is not ade-quately addressed over a prolonged period, allowance is thereby made for the emergence of a catastrophic threat to the viability of democracy as we have understood it. Although the viability of any democracy is *always* being challenged at some level, America has not faced a serious structural or conceptual threat within its homeland since the Civil War. I do not believe we are facing such a threat today (in terms of our democracy itself), yet I am disturbed by the maturation of numerous contradictions, one of which is exemplified in the Islamic religious school in D.C. More particularly, I am concerned for the potential of radical Islamic militancy among the African-American underclass. The November 27 issue of the *Wall Street Journal* related the statements of a young African-American inmate in a state prison in California. The statements of the inmate reflect a long-evolving attitude and worldview shared by a growing number of frustrated, inner-city Blacks: "[The inmate] says the hijackers were justified in attacking the WTC. As the embodiment of American economic power, the twin towers were a military rather than a civilian target, he says. 'My first reaction was, "God has found the answer to my prayers.'" . . . He says about one-third of the prison's [several hundred] Muslim inmates agree with him on this point. 'America is not the great place everybody cracks it up to be,' he says."

I should inform the reader that this particular prison, in Vacaville, is fairly soft as far as prisons go. The harsher penitentiaries (Corcoran, Lancaster, Pelican Bay, etc.) house a much higher percentage of more militant and hard-care, nihilistic inmates.

America has ignored the African-American ghetto tinderbox for a very long time. I have no intention of attempting an extended analysis, as the situation is extremely complex and acutely sensitive, and such an effort on my part would surely be inadequate as well as a distraction from the very limited focal range of my essay. Yet if I had the ability to stimulate just one genre of discussion on a national scale, it would be precisely this.

Historically, as a general rule from at least the third decade of the twentieth century, our nation has tended to be less proactive than reactive in the face of rising threats. I suppose this is an inevitable tendency for an advanced democracy in a highly materialistic culture. We deeply enjoy our frivolities and choose to assume the danger just beyond the horizon will remain there. In this case, the rising threat is not so far away that only a skilled visionary could observe its form and magnitude. The inner cities are a cauldron of frustration boiling just beneath the surface of the American public image—just *barely beneath the surface.*

A crusade of Islamic militancy could set off an explosion that would not, as have previous outbursts (1965, 1968, 1992, etc.), be restricted to the inner cities. Middle-class America would be recovering for a long time from such a conflagration.

An overwhelming majority of African-American Muslims have had no genuine metaphysical encounter (that is obvious from their behavior and their overall conversation).

Islam is for them a protest statement. This is similar to the communist Black Panther movement in the late 1960s, in which angry young Blacks embraced an ideology that they had no genuine admiration for, and that very few of them even understood. The Panthers' embrace of communism was a formal repudiation of the core values of a nation that they felt would never allow them a meaningful share in the franchise.

In spite of the increasing number of successful Black Americans over the past several decades (as exemplified dramatically in the inner circle of the current federal administration), this despairing sense of exclusion has not diminished as a general experience in the ghettos of America. (There are certainly *many* exceptions to this rule, but the pool of danger is among the millions who are not the exceptions.) This discontent has led to a spreading nihilism (fueled by the consequences of the War on Drugs more than by any other outside source-factor), and the psychological conditions are ripe for an organized mass movement of anti-American militancy among the Black underclass. These are not the kind of people from whom suicide bombers are made, nor would the precepts of Sharia ever have a serious chance of widespread acceptance in the sensuous and materialistic ghetto culture. But the anti-Americanism of Islamic militancy is the central potential inducement that, when mingled with the violent gangster culture, would promise to threaten America with a civil crisis of proportions unknown since the middle of the nineteenth century.

Apart from a concerted effort to effectively address this inner-city discontent, I fear this ghetto rage will eventually fuse with anti-American Islamic radicalism (absent a meaningful commitment to Sharia law), and that it will explode across our land with horrific intensity.

The perception of hopeless disenfranchisement has been radicalized by the drug policies of the U.S. government, which are widely viewed in the ghetto as a calculated war against minorities rather than an actual war against drugs. The accuracy or inaccuracy of this perception is not relevant to the danger at hand. People act on their perceptions, and the consensus-perception among angry African-Americans is that the U.S. government willfully calibrates its socio-economic and its penal-judicial policies against the welfare of the Black community.

The sense of disenfranchisement and oppression is the principal exploitative factor in the appeal of Islamic radicalism. In his Special Report for the October 15 issue of *Newsweek,* Fareed Zakaria quoted from Fouad Ajami's seminal work, *The Arab Predicament:* "The fundamentalist call has resonance because it invited men to participate . . . [in] contrast to a political culture that reduces citizens to spectators and asks them to leave things to their rulers." Zakaria adds his own important observation: "Fundamentalism gave Arabs who were dissatisfied with their lot a powerful language of opposition."

For an angry and frustrated man in the ghetto, having bought into the nihilistic gangster culture and the unredeemable logic of victimhood, the appeal of actively belonging to an international, anti-American revolutionary movement is dizzying in its effect. In hitching his wagon to this rising star, he has experienced the apotheosis. He is no longer a common thug sought after by the local police, but is now a person of dimensions on the radar of the CIA and the FBI. How many enraged, nihilistic, inner-city gangster wannabes would turn this down?

The sleepers who have come to sow this destruction in our land have melted inconspicuously into the Arab-American Islamic community. The leadership of this community has not been impressive in its assurances to America that it will clean up its house, and does not seem sincere in acknowledging that its house needs cleaning at all. The U.S. Islamic leadership's overriding, publicly expressed concern has not been in the direction of helping our government prevent another major terrorist attack, but rather of rebuking America for looking suspiciously at the Western Islamic community (as if we have no legitimate reasons for our anxiety!). *The Economist,* generally less hamstrung than the mainstream U.S. media by obsessions with political correctness, was bold in observing: "[The U.S.] has been unable to engage Islamic countries in a serious debate about how Mr. bin Laden has abused the Koran for his own ends. It has not sent any Muslim Americans or Afghan-Americans to make its case. This is partly because groups close to the administration, such as the American Muslim Council and the Council on American Islamic Relations (CAIR), have been far more concerned about American criticism of Muslims than about acts of terror in the name of Islam (CAIR's founder said the trial of those found guilty of the 1993 attack on the World Trade Centre was a 'travesty of justice')" (November 10).

No reasonable person is suggesting that all Muslims are terrorists, or even that a substantial percentage of Western Muslims are terrorists. Yet when terrorist activities are accomplished by those who are traced consistently to a certain milieu, we must negotiate with that setting for a more effective cooperation. A carefully applied measure of pressure is not inconsistent with our national philosophy. Someone has said: "The Bill of Rights is not a suicide pact."

We might remind ourselves of the brief preamble to the Constitution of the United States: "We, the People of the United States, in order to form a more perfect union, establish justice, ensure domestic tranquility, *provide for the common defence,* promote the *general welfare,* and secure the blessings of liberty to ourselves and our posterity, do ordain and establish this Constitution for the United States of America" (emphasis mine).

The spectacular array of individual rights delineated

in the Constitution is *subservient to* the collective welfare of the nation. If an enhanced surveillance is imposed on a setting undeniably associated with the program of terrorism against the United States, that milieu has a distorted and shallow understanding of the Constitution if it believes its rights are infringed by this surveillance. Not only is an unlimited and unconditional investigation of such a milieu endorsed by the Constitution, but the government's failure to sufficiently investigate and surveil that milieu would be a violation of the collective values that the Constitution was written to uphold.

It is within our means to institute a new magnitude of capacity for homeland security without compromising, in any fundamental way, the framework of ideals that has guided our nation since its founding.

Also, if military tribunals promise to more swiftly and comprehensively extract vital information necessary to "the common defence" of our homeland, and if these tribunals promise to more efficiently administer a commensurate measure of justice toward murderers involved in the international campaign to destroy America, the U.S. Constitution is firmly on the side of a discretionary use of these tribunals. Mr. Ashcroft attested, with no apologies, in an interview published in the December 12 issue of *Newsweek:* "This [decision to set up military tribunals] is a tool that the president should have in the arsenal of democracy designed to thwart and to counter the terrorist war on the United States."

Rather than "shredding the Constitution," Mr. Ashcroft's support for handing over non-citizen terrorists to the Ministry of Defense is an act of supreme regard for the program outlined in that document. Is the Attorney General ruthless in this counter-campaign against the terrorist program? He had better be. He was hired to run the U.S. Ministry of Justice, not the Red Cross. Justice for America, at the present moment, is the annihilation of the Islamic terrorist movement and the crippling punishment of all who have supported it. In this particular attorney general, we have an old-fashioned G-man who is quite up to that task.

The love of America and its higher values, combined with an informed appreciation of the broader aims of the U.S. Constitution, should effectively mitigate any discomfort we might feel toward this aggressive battlefield tactic. Military tribunals are a battlefield operation. A softening of this operation is a compromise on the battlefield and is therefore a compromise of the national security that our Constitution was written to uphold.

Intellectual and emotional sophistication confers an ability to traverse various conceptual subsystems without suffering a confusion of perspective. The U.S. Constitution is a remarkable constellation of subsystems organized into a unified document serving as a manual for the success of democracy. If we allow our enemies to use our Constitution to their own advantage, this is due to no inherent weakness in the Constitution itself, but rather to our own lack of emotional maturity and intellectual discipline.

The Constitution is a generative entity rather than a petrified stack of papers. The most recent Amendment occasioned by a national crisis was ratified in 1971, endowing U.S. citizens with the right to vote from the age of eighteen rather than twenty-one. The Vietnam War was instrumental in this recent constitutional development. The jungles of blood were imported into every American living room, and the government's inability to articulate a convincing justification for the daily slaughter of American boys fresh out of high school led to an outpouring of public support for the dignity of younger people. If they were old enough to fight and die for this country, surely they were old enough to have a say in who would lead this country.

Prior to the crisis-related Amendment of 1971, the

most recent development within the Constitution had been ratified in 1967. It concerned the procedure for succession to the vice presidency, and was occasioned by the national crisis of November 22, 1963. Running the American democracy is a constant fine-tuning process, and our Constitution will continue developing as we move from crisis to crisis, negotiating with the imperatives of each new era and triumphing over contradictions that can no longer be ignored. I believe our nation needs to debate the viability of an Amendment that would create a broad legal subsystem for terrorist-related issues, one that would include such a loss of civil advantages for a conviction on terrorist charges that the criminal appeal of the terrorist movement would be painfully damaged.

We have an abundance of historical experiences to draw from. Our history assures us that we are capable of developing effective checks and balances to condition an enhanced latitude for our security apparatus. Nothing is foolproof on an absolute scale, yet the genius of the American system involves a fertility of logic enabling us to approximate a reasonable balance among contending interests. In an age of knowledge and mass travel, we need to know our government has not lost control. Even when the last al Qaeda stronghold has imploded, the nature of the new epoch is such that our homeland security system can never safely return to the relative casualness of September 10.

We still have many contradictions to contend with, and many immaturities to outgrow. But our negotiations with the twenty-first century will succeed if we maintain the national philosophy that is tried and proven. Our triumphant national philosophy has always been, and must always be, a complementarity of Ideology and Realpolitik.

17.   Consequences of Economic Decline

Another successful terrorist assault would threaten to induce an economic disintegration leading to unprecedented waves of crime and unpredictable damage to the national spirit.

In January 2001, the Bush economic team was handed a solid economy (although the surge that had continued throughout the Clinton years was subsiding). Less than a year later, unemployment is at a thirty-year high, diving interest rates are hammering fragile retirement programs, and the country is in its first official recession since 1992. If the terrorist threat is to be even partially blamed for this, then we have another compelling reason for pursuing a *swift elimination* of this threat. However unpleasant and impolitic it might be, the situation requires a dramatic elevation in our level of strategy.

As the country endures the ongoing strain and uncertainty of the terrorist threat, it will need a superior economic strategy and a presidential team capable of inspiring confidence. Perhaps the economy can pull itself up by the bootstraps—we have sufficient resources for that. But another successful terrorist attack would threaten to undermine even our attempt at an economic recovery, and would likely leave the current team completely overwhelmed by the challenge.

Due to the effectiveness of the national ministries headed by Messrs. Rumsfeld, Ashcroft, Tenet, and Mueller, the terrorist network has so far been unable to execute a follow-up strike to its perverse success on September 11. If the enemy does succeed eventually, whether by conventional or unconventional devices of destruction, how well will our economy withstand the assault? It is imperative that we end this war swiftly, regardless of how impolitic the nature and scale of our attack might be.

By every meaningful standard of measurement in the

real world of human relations, we as a nation are fully justified in holding hostage and, if necessary, completely sacri-
ficing the spiritual landmarks most dear to the terrorists and
their tens of millions of sympathizers. If such an effective
measure were taken by our government, the moral responsibility for the destruction would lay with the Islamic community of the Middle East that has generated, tolerated,
financed, applauded, and prayed for the success of their terrorist brethren. Such an action would bring us no more into
fault than did the firebombing of Dresden. We cannot be
held hostage to the unfortunate realities of collateral
destruction when our country is faced with the threat of
mayhem by Middle Eastern citizens who may have devices
capable of replicating or even superseding the destruction of
September 11. There is simply no such thing as a clean military response to an act of war. Even the great war conducted
by The Greatest Generation was far from clean.

18. Open and Accountable Government

The principle of open and accountable government is indispensable to the maintenance of our democracy. Our representatives must know what goes on, and the press must be ubiquitous.

Our government system was built on the realist assumption of human nature's inclination toward aggression and abuse. Jonathan Turley commented in the December 14 issue of the *Los Angeles Times:* "Madison built a constitutional system without romance based on a frank understanding of the inclinations of free people. He rejected the unguarded optimism of human nature as the guarantee of good government. 'If men were angels,' Madison noted, 'no government would be necessary.' Madison built a system that could be governed by devils and still function."

People will tend to get away with what they can. Our founding fathers developed a model of government based on the assumption that human nature requires a steadfast check on its darker impulses. The fortification of "checks and balances," enhanced by the watchful private eyes of a free press, is crucial to the maintenance of this model. Our support of the president and his administration, and our confidence in the government's ability to get the job done, does not imply a blind trust in the people who run our government. The success of America has always depended on an unwillingness to subscribe to such gullibility.

I have endeavored to illustrate the legitimacy of public support for our government as it directs the resources of America toward a comprehensive success in this war against a sub-world of Islamic terrorists. My arguments in support of the government have been unwavering and, hopefully, have provided some meaningful intellectual content. If the reader were to suspect me of being an Establishment sycophant, this eighteenth and final article is likely to dispel that notion.

Due to the strength and robust greatness of our nation, we tend to be more constitutionally fit than other nations to engage in profound and honest self-criticism. In looking self-critically at ourselves and our history (which only a strong and confident people can do), we affirm that the embarrassing episodes are not the defining statements of our civilization. We affirm this by our openness to criticism and by the gradual triumph of transparency over opacity. The laurel wreath for this triumph cannot be handed to the government itself, which naturally tends to prefer opacity, but rather to the Americans who have stood on the principles of democracy and refused to allow our government to violate these principles.

I trust the abilities of our leaders. I have confidence in the resources of America and in its system of government. Do I trust the leaders themselves? Yes, for as far as my representatives can see them. The House of Representatives and a free and roving press are the eyes we have for seeing what the Executive Branch of our government is doing. Our representatives, if they are to actually represent us in a meaningful way, must have access, deep and broad, to the inner workings of the Executive Branch (to the extent of what is reasonable). The press, if it is to serve effectively in the defense and evolution of democracy, must be disciplined, savvy, and aggressive.

My extensive quoting from a wide array of journalists and other media sources is an effort to promote the value of a free and variegated press. I certainly have my complaints about some of the philosophical leanings of the media in general, yet I recognize the imperative democratic principle of a free and aggressive domestic army of watchers. The press, to speak in a peculiar but meaningful fashion, is an internal ministry of defense, on guard against hostile intrusions into the domain of democracy.

The press and the government (meaning, in this context, the Executive Branch) will never find a happy center. The nature of democracy seemingly consigns them to a perpetual tug-of-war. As our democracy has matured, the government has tended to be occupied less and less by genuine, statesmen-like figures, and more and more by purified political entities. Unfortunately, this tendency accrues from the very nature of an advanced democracy, and is a swelling contradiction that is likely to resolve itself, somewhere in the misty future, in a fundamental transformation of the American social contract. As our democracy moves inexorably in that direction, the press will need to sustain its aggression and hone its discipline as the interior defense against the threat of a runaway government.

The recent media emphasis on military tribunals has obscured the truly disconcerting decisions by the president— most notably on November 1 and December 13—to block public and even congressional access to presidential documents from previous administrations. Since the Bush administration has offered no convincing justification for this extreme exercise of "executive privilege," America is effectively being told, "Trust us. We are honest people." Although we certainly hope it is true that honest people are running our government, a willingness to blindly trust the leadership would be dangerously naïve on our part. To quote again from Jonathan Turley: "Madison built a constitutional system without romance based on a frank understanding of the inclination of free people. He rejected the unguarded optimism of human nature as the guarantee of good government." We should also recall the maxims of Mr. Reagan and Ms. Thatcher:

"Trust, but verify"—Ronald Reagan.
"You can never let down your guard"—Margaret Thatcher.

We should trust our government, insofar as we can

verify the truthfulness of what it tells us. I am hardly suggesting President Bush is engaging in dishonesty with the
American public. But he is doing a good job of creating sus-
picions in this direction. Emily Levine, writing in the
December 11 issue of the *Los Angeles Times*, provided a very
honest, non-assailing, and gently worded response to the president's decision of November 1: "When I read that President
Bush had issued an executive order enabling him to bar pub-
lication of the records of the Reagan administration—an
administration in which, coincidentally, Bush's father was
vice president—I wonder if there is something in those papers
that makes George H.W. Bush look bad. When the government doesn't trust me, I don't trust the government."

Ms. Levine is not accusing the government of a
cover-up. She is respectfully stating her honest response to
this seemingly suspicious activity by the president.

Access to these papers is significant for the welfare
of America. The president's decision deprives us of a better
understanding of how the world really works, and dimin-
ishes our opportunities for learning how to avoid a repeat of
past mistakes. Is this particular invocation of executive privilege a drastic measure taken with a view to the interests of
America's welfare, *or* to the personal, self-interested secrets
of several government leaders? We do not know, but historical precedents of this sort are not so encouraging.

Joan Claybrook, president of Public Citizen, was
quoted in the *Los Angeles Times* as saying: "Bush's executive order violates not only the spirit but the letter of the
law" (November 20). Whatever the truth of the matter, it is
not to the advantage of America that the president has created this perception.

The same article also observed: "Rather than ensur-
ing open access to presidential records [which the law was
designed to provide], the order drew a veil of secrecy over
them. . . The Nov. 1 order also extended this secrecy rule

to 'vice presidential records.' This gives the current president the power to block the public release of files from the office of former vice President George Bush, his father."

The *Times'* official editorial was fairly blunt: "The administration's 'just trust us' campaign has failed" (December 11).

When our Congress is expressing an unusual level of frustration over what it perceives as a pattern of presidential abuse of the "executive privilege," we should pay very close attention. We should hope the press would aggressively pursue its role as our eyes and ears, using its access and its constitutional mandate to guard America against secretive encroachments upon the principles of our democracy. Rather than being a failure to support the president, the media's refusal to allow for even the beginnings of a runaway presidency would be an act of supreme support for the president, since human nature is such that it grows dangerously vulnerable when deprived of adequate, external checks and balances. Walter Bagehot observed in the October 13 issue of *The Economist:* "Too much prating about loyalty, even in war, damages democracy's health."

During World War II, as President Roosevelt enjoyed overwhelming public and congressional support for the war against the Axis powers, the Senate Republican Leader Robert Taft declared: "Criticism in a time of war is essential to the maintenance of any kind of democratic government." Albert R. Hunt observed in the December 13 issue of the *Wall Street Journal:* "The great Ohio conservative continued to assail President Roosevelt's domestic policies through much of World War II, and was one of the few politicians with the courage to speak out against the internment of Japanese-Americans."

War, along with high approval ratings, cannot be allowed as a cover for encroachments on democratic principles such as accountability, the separation of powers, and the rule of law.

This concern about a swelling Executive Branch is also being expressed in England toward the Blair administration (although hardly on the same scale). *The Economist* observed in its November 17 issue: "Labour's lead over the Conservatives in the [MORI] opinion poll was, at 32%, higher than at any time since just after it first came to power in 1997. . . Some of its recent actions suggest that since its re-election last June it has become increasingly intolerant of dissent and exasperated with institutions— from the judiciary to Parliament itself—that seek to check its powers. . . David Blunkett has added to the overall impression that this is a government that does as it pleases and brooks no criticism. . . [Some of the government's recent policy decisions] look typical of the errors that administrations begin to make once they come to consider themselves invulnerable."

As a matter of historical, empirical fact, high approval ratings tend to lure a government in the direction of executive abuse. Both the ubiquity of the press and the principle of the separation of powers must be guarded with vigilance, particularly in times of war. Gail R. Pontuto of Secane, Pennsylvania, wrote to the editor of *Newsweek:* "The separation of powers in America is fundamental to the way I and many other Americans see our government" (December 10).

When Mr. Bush was declared the winner of the presidential election, it was refreshing to witness his sense of awe toward the office he would now be filling. This sense of profound respect for the office of the presidency was much in need of restoration after the prolific lack of such respect shown by the previous administration. We should hope that our current president will sustain this personal sense of awe for the office of the presidency, and will work effectively to restore to this office the moral prestige and even the mystical aura lost in recent national tragedies such as the Vietnam War, Watergate, Iran-Contra, and the incalculable moral disasters of the Clinton era.

Yet our steadfast support for President Bush should not be allowed to translate into an endorsement of executive abuse under cover of a ninety-percent approval rating and a war of nerve-wracking uncertainty.

The *Los Angeles Times* reported in its December 14 issue:

> President Bush on Thursday [December 13] withheld from Congress an array of documents *sought by lawmakers* in cases ranging from Clinton-era fund-raising scandals to a decades-old murder in Boston, provoking outrage *from Republicans and Democrats alike. . .*
>
> Bush already is at odds with Congress over the White House's refusal to release details on Vice President Dick Cheney's energy task force that drafted the administration's energy legislation behind closed doors and on potential conflict-of-interest information involving the investments of Bush's senior White House political advisor Karl Rove [regarding Rove's stock holdings in the now-disgraced and bankrupt Enron].
>
> Bush also angered historians by issuing an executive order to restrict public access to the papers of retired presidents. . . "Everyone [in Congress] is in agreement you guys are making a big mistake," [senior *Republican* House member Dan] Burton told Justice Department lawyers. . . "The legislative branch has oversight responsibility to make sure there is no corruption in the executive branch."

Representative Henry A. Waxman was quoted in that same *Times* article: "Clearly, there's an emerging pattern of a sense that [the Bush administration] can operate without the public or the Congress having the opportunity to see what's going on. This is troubling because governments should be transparent."

Public concerns are being voiced in spite of the wartime conditions of patriotism and support for the president. David Katzner of Woodland Hills, California, wrote to the editor of the *Los Angeles Times:* "[The president presses] full steam ahead with a missile defense shield no one wants and invokes executive privilege, keeping damning evidence about his secret energy negotiations from congressional investigators. . . The spin the White House put on the executive privilege order was nothing short of astounding" (December 17). And from Dan Freedland of Rolling Hills Estates, California: "Bush has, by most accounts, done a good job of prosecuting the war on terrorism. . . [But his] arrogance and disregard for the right of the public to know has crippled the foundation of our free society [note: Mr. Freedland weakens his argument by this flight of verbal exaggeration]. . . The Enron scandal is irrevocably intertwined with the highest Bush administration officials, most of whom profited handsomely while the worker bees helplessly watched their retirement funds evaporate. Enron's Ken Lay had privileged access to the Cheney energy policy discussions. And of course, Vice President Cheney refuses to disclose any information about their meetings."

Over the past ten years, Ken Lay and other Enron executives have donated nearly $2 million toward the political advancement of George W. Bush, along with Lay's donations of over $300,000 in soft money to the Republican Party and his wife's donation of $100,000 for the Bush inauguration festivities. Donations on this scale can hardly be viewed as "good-will offerings." We should not be so naïve as to assume that political donations running into the six- and seven-digit figures are anything less than calculated business investments.

It is also known that Karl Rove owned up to a quarter-million dollars of Enron stock, and that Larry Lindsay and Robert B. Zoellick "went straight from Enron's payroll to their federal jobs" (quoted from Robert Scheer in the *Los Angeles Times*, December 11).

One hundred million dollars was spent on Mr. Bush's presidential campaign. People do not donate such sums of money because of their fondness for another person. These are business investments. America would be justified in requesting a straightforward listing of all the major contributors to the Bush campaign, with specific amounts included in the listing, and a cross referencing of these donations with the financial benefits to each company accruing from specific policy decisions made by the president. This should be most emphatically required in the matter of the space-based missile defense system (SBMDS).

Senator John McCain, in an interview for the September 27 issue of *The Rolling Stone*, admitted to the delinquent role of donations in major U.S. policy decisions: "I can tell you that, in everything we do in Washington, the power and influence of big money and special interests fundamentally dictate our agenda. . . I'm saying we're all affected by it—including myself."

How much do Raytheon, Boeing, Lockheed Martin, General Dynamics, and Northrop Grumman stand to gain financially from the U.S. government's pursuit of an SBMDS? Americans have a right to know this, since their tax money is footing the entire bill.

I fully support our government's pursuit of this missile-defense system, although I do not believe it would actually be effective in shooting down missiles.

The MDS would cost tens of billions of dollars to

build, and billions more to maintain. If we succeed in building it, would it really work? If it worked, would it actually be relevant to the nuclear threats confronting us?

In terms of a real-world missile defense, I believe it is the ultimate Maginot Line. In terms of what is motivating the costly pursuit of this line, I believe it is a massive kickback scheme and an ego trip. Yet I support it one hundred percent for the consequential advantages it will confer on America. This pursuit of an SBMDS will secure our national advantage over the most important real-estate frontier of the twenty-first century: space.

Economically, psychologically, and militarily, the domination of space is the imperative of advantage in the twenty-first century.

This program will not break us economically. Of the approximately $100 billion spent on the project, much will find its way back into the economy directly, and much indirectly, so that we should not imagine that this $100 billion will be buried in a miser's back yard. (Also, if we choose to do so, we could pay for this many times over by giving up the bureaucratic snafu called "The War on Drugs." This program squanders billions annually in a fashion that actually brings further damage to our economy and sends billions more into the foreign coffers of drug producers and international narcotics dealers.) Most importantly, the MDS project promises to result in technological developments that could have revolutionary effects on the structure of commerce and security, and perhaps even on political organization and cultural philosophies. This is the extraordinary lesson of the 1960's ARPANET project (which led to Al Gore's invention of the Internet—ah, just a bit of levity in this much-too-serious book).

If we do not pursue this SBMDS, a coalition of other nations eventually will. I am not suggesting the MDS project is a *good* thing. I am merely insisting it is historically necessary for America to pursue this. From this perspective, since pulling out of the ABM Treaty was a prerequisite to the pursuit of the necessary technologies, our president did what had to be done.

At the same time, Americans are entitled to a transparent exposé of the straightforward relationships between corporate advantage, taxpayer dollars, and major U.S. policy decisions (foreign and domestic). Our representatives and the press have both the constitutional and the popular mandate for this, and they are positioned to accomplish it.

What is a viable global vision for America? Our government needs to deliver on this, and yet it cannot do so without the presence and input of the public. Free debate and civilized public criticism are indispensable to the democratic process. Dale F. Eickelman observed in the December 9 issue of the *Los Angeles Times:* "Public opinion is easier to hijack in the absence of full debate."

To encourage us in refusing the lazy naïveté of a blind trust in our leaders, we should consider that the current crisis confronting our nation is largely the result of a catastrophic failure of leadership, at the highest levels of the U.S. government, over the past decade.

Mansoor Ijaz, a member of the Council on Foreign Relations, publicly testified from his first-hand experience in attempting to address the escalating terrorist problem through the 1990s: "Clinton's failure to grasp the opportunity to unravel increasingly organized extremists, coupled with [National Security Advisor Sandy] Berger's assessments of their potential to directly threaten the U.S., represents one of the most serious foreign policy failures in American history" (*Los Angeles Times,* December 5).

Staunch loyalists of the former president swiftly mounted a typical spin in response to Ijaz's disclosure. But we have been down this road with them before, on far too many occasions. Ijaz's testimony is worthy of a serious evaluation.

Most importantly, the disclosures are a further stimulus for the American public to forcefully insist on more consistent government transparency and a more serious involvement of civilian debate in the major policy decisions of the country.

Public criticism and free debate are a high order for our time. Rush Limbaugh wrote for the October 4 issue of the *Wall Street Journal:* "We have no choice but to address the policies and decisions, made at the very highest level of our government, which helped bring us to this point."

Our government *needs* the civilized but aggressive involvement of the public.

Conclusion

Until we effect a change in the psychological structure of those who hope to destroy America, the terrorist movement, although wounded and staggering, will continue replicating leaders, plans, and recruits. We are currently *hampering* the efforts of our enemies, but we are no nearer to *eliminating* this threat than when the campaign first began. Why should we choose to drag this war on for many years, suffering the distraction and the diversion of our resources in a drawn-out marathon, with the years to come routinely punctuated by successful terrorist strikes and the anxiety of heightened national alerts? Our enemies do not merit such a sacrifice from us. It is within our means to go aggressively to the marrow, and to attack the generative substance of the movement that has pledged itself and the name of its god to our destruction.

The militants construe this entire situation as a religious war. They interpret their successes in recent years as evidence that their god will bless and reward their efforts to destroy non-Islamic civilization, beginning with Israel and America. Jerrold M. Post observed in the December 9 Opinion Section of the *Los Angeles Times:* "The defeat of the Soviet Union, a superpower, was confirmation that Allah was on their side."

So long as we allow them to continue believing this, the threat of mass murder and mayhem at the hands of Islamic militants will remain a dominant fixture in our lives.

The militants have called on Muslims to "uphold their religion" by attacking American interests. As an al Qaeda leader challenged: "Allah says fight. . . The American interests are everywhere, all over the world. Every Muslim has to play his real and true role to uphold his religion." And the October sermon by bin Laden: "Allah has blessed a group of vanguard Muslims, the forefront of Islam, to destroy America. . . Every Muslim has to rush to make his religion victorious. . . I swear to Allah that America will not live in peace."

"Every Muslim has to rush to make his religion victorious. . . Every Muslim has to play his real and true role to uphold his religion." The fatal vulnerability of the terrorist mass movement is precisely this link in its psychology between its military success on the ground and its confidence in the favor of Allah. This confidence will be destroyed only by means of a devastating series of losses on the ground. A synchronized military effort, involving Israel and an alliance of northern powers, simultaneously targeting the regime of Saddam Hussein and the terrorists' theological landmarks in Saudi Arabia and Jerusalem, would promise to swiftly accomplish this destruction in the psychology of the militant movement.

After witnessing the massacres on September 11, the California inmate confessed: "Allah has found an answer to my prayers."

By denying any further answers to their prayers, and by erasing from existence the very site toward which they pray, we will have shown our military capacity to be stronger than their concept of God. In such a demonstration of truth in the real world, we will have vanquished the ground on which the militant psychology is built.

My argument does not suggest that such a measure would compel every terrorist to lay down his guns, or that our current measures of aggression against this threat would thereby be rendered unnecessary. The mopping-up operation would still require a significant effort, but the war *in principle* would be over. The truly hard-core terrorists among them, such as bin Laden himself (if he is alive), have so completely invested their souls in this campaign that nothing short of death will likely ever end the threat they pose to the human race. But this truly hard-core element would utterly lose its support base, and its recruitment program would hit a brick wall. The remaining, committed terrorists would be isolated, hounded, and subject to betrayal by those who had once idolized them. For al Qaeda members who have committed no terrorist acts, a full amnesty could be offered in return for a complete debriefing. The heroes would become the goats, and we could begin applying our resources toward a program along the lines of a multi-tiered Marshall Plan.

But until we dismantle the militant theology by bringing this holy war to a showdown (a spectacular and decisive showdown), the threat to our security and to our prosperity will remain.

Michael Vlahos explained in his article for the November 8 issue of *The Rolling Stone:* "The enemy measures its strength [most emphatically, the strength of its god] in battle . . . and finds in battle personal apotheosis [glorification]. We must rob our opponents of this realization."

The militants, linking their concept of God to the campaign of terror, will not be dissuaded until this concept is radically adjusted.

Murama Takaji, the twenty-two-year-old prospective kamikaze pilot, boasted several weeks after Pearl Harbor: "It would be a great honor to crash into an American ship. I hear there are many pretty geishas in the next life."

Murama's god had promised him such things. Our controlled display of violence in August 1945 adjusted Murama's concept of God and eliminated the Japanese fascination with suicide attacks against the United States. Since that summer fifty-six years ago, the Japanese have not sent a single soldier into combat. Our bullets, flame-throwers, and 500-pound TNT bombs did not do this. Nikolay Palchikoff, an observer in Hiroshima after the bomb had been dropped, wrote for the December 3 issue of *Newsweek:* "There were images of bodies burned like photographic negatives into the concrete and an utter silence so psychologically traumatic that it would be 40 years before I ever spoke about it."

A deeply disturbing thing had been done on that summer morning in Japan. Yet it was a measure that spared the world any further terrors from the most militaristic and necrophilic civilization on earth. It was so long ago that the intensity of the shock has been largely forgotten. The Islamic militants have boasted that "the myth of the superpower is dead." John Keehan observed in the November 27 issue of the *Wall Street Journal:* "There has been talk of a "Fifty-Years War" on terrorism. In truth it may last far longer than that. Until militant Islam . . . [has] been *terrified into passivity,* this war will continue" (emphasis mine).

Our current terms of engagement may require fifty years or longer to conclude this war and eliminate this threat to the safety of Americans throughout the world. Most likely, this threat will never be eliminated on the strength of our current approach, and history would judge us harshly for such a failure. In contrast, the Americans of that heroic generation preceding us did what needed to be done, however unpleasant and impolitic, and they did not hand to *us* an unfinished job.

We have the capacity to abruptly "terrify into passivity" the twenty-first century kamikaze enthusiasts. We must create a vision for them, one so terrifying that the theological concepts that undergird and inspire their movement will collapse "into an utter silence." This would not make us feel good, but it would make our enemies feel very bad, and in such a vision the idea of martyrdom can only lose its appeal. There could be no apotheosis in such a loss.

The formula advanced in this book is not suggested as a stand-alone panacea, but rather as the principal strategy to be supplemented by everything else we are currently doing. E. J. Dionne Jr. observed in the October 1 issue of the *Post Weekly:* "We need to debate which forms of war will prove effective and which won't."

This book is my contribution to the debate.

Postscript:
December 17, 2001

On the evening of October 26, I was on my way to dinner when a friend approached and informed me of yet another outbreak of anthrax. As we parted, his haunting comment was: "So it's spreading." As I stood at the top of a staircase surveying the rolling hills in a setting sun, I wondered how the great Americans of our past might respond if they could see the distress afflicting our country—Washington, Jefferson, Harriet Beecher Stowe, Lincoln, FDR, John Kennedy, and Martin Luther King. A galaxy of names and faces seemed to line the hills. I watched as the gold of evening gave place to the darkness of night, and then went inside for a meal that seemed to have no taste. With no deliberate effort on my part, it occurred to me that the generative marrow of the enemy corpus would be eliminated only by an invocation of America's ultimate destructive capacity. It was not a pleasant thought, but it raced through my mind with provocative animation and gave me an integrating focus. Later that night, as I was attempting to continue my work on a series of studies that has occupied me for the past several years, the pressure of my conceptual experience at the table shouted down my thoughts on the studies. I set the materials aside, grabbed my clipboard, and rapidly made a list of several dozen observations for development. My resolve has not wavered over the past eight weeks, and I am grateful for the patience of my friends as they tolerated my focus on this endeavor.

In the course of this book, my trivialization of "good and evil" is due to the incontestable fact of the amoral nature of international affairs. Ideally, good and evil *should be* the determining factor in *every human calculus,* whether in war or outside of war. But we do not live in an ideal world. An idealistic approach to world relationships would place us at a disadvantage leading eventually to our destruction. Robert D. Kaplan explained in a polite understatement: "Now we are truly in an age of new technological threats . . . that will return us to . . . [a time] when realism flourished under men like John Adams and Alexander Hamilton. . . Such realism posits that foreign affairs entail a separate, sadder morality than the kind we apply in domestic policy and in our daily lives. That is because domestically we operate under the rule of law, while the wider world is an anarchic realm where we are forced to take the law into our own hands" (*The Post Weekly,* October 1).

The structure of our reasoning will vary accordingly with the differing realms of life. In this book my reasoning is calibrated to the realm of war. It is hardly my favorite subject, but our enemies have shoved it in our face.

I am a Christian, an evangelical. My faith assures me of my responsibility to this nation and to its system of government. The Bible instructs me in the complexities of life, and thus in the shifting requirements of the various seasons. There is a time for building up, and a time for tearing down. Each season has its own set of rules. On other scales of analysis, my observations would certainly alienate many who might concur with me in the stricter context of the issue at hand.

In distinguishing one sphere of obligation from another, I am reminded of the great NFL pass rusher, Reggie White. Mr. White is a Christian who is quite vocal with his confession. Off the field, he is not shy about challenging other members of his team, exhorting them to give a more serious view to the issues. But in the game, he has a common objective with ten other athletes. The ball is snapped, the players rush. Regardless of the competing worldviews, religions, and moral persuasions, in *the context of the game* their efforts are coordinated by a strict and common logic. Mr. White, a peace-loving and compassionate man, deploys his formidable and frightening physical power against the unfortunate man with the ball. The man he later prays for is the one he has just lifted from the ground and hurled down with a painful thud. That was his job at the moment, and it was done with the full measure of his strength. No quarterback ever benefited from Reggie White's pulpit pieties.

I have neither an athletic ability nor a greatness of personal character on a par with Reggie White, but I am able to appreciate the complexity of reality and to distinguish one set of requirements from another. A system of valid logic in one situation does not necessarily apply in another. My disturbing grief at the sight of weeping Palestinian schoolchildren stands side by side, yet does not mingle with, my calculation of what must be done to destroy the spiritual inspiration of the terrorist mass movement. My doctrine of peace and forgiveness is not compromised by, and does not interfere with, my logic of destruction aimed against an organized enemy seeking to cripple my country.

In a "Review & Outlook" article from its September 13 issue, the *Wall Street Journal*'s editorial observed: "It means real war. . . It also means rethinking some of the softer political pieties about our modern, violent world."

An ability to be dangerous is the bedrock of truth in international affairs. History knows of no era in which this was not so. And if we wish to persuade ourselves that human nature is outgrowing these timeless amoral realities, we must first persuade ourselves that the twentieth century did not really happen.

Ralph Peters wrote in the October 1 issue of the *Post Weekly:* "Despite their defiant rhetoric, we would do well not to underestimate the underlying fear our enemies have of our power. . . The humanitarianism we cherish is regarded as a sign of impotence by such opponents."

Although America has dominated much of the world for over half a century, as a civilization we are still in our ascendancy. The efficiency of our system and the success of our power have combined to revive a conviction "lost somewhere in the rice paddies of Vietnam." History has conferred a destiny. It is the hour of democracy's triumph and America was handed the torch. Robert L. Bartley wrote in a high-stakes conclusion to his November 19 article in the *Wall Street Journal:* "The civilization reaching back to the Mayflower is recovering its self-confidence, lost somewhere in the rice paddies of Vietnam. . . The U.S. has the power to shape the future, and is on the verge of acquiring the will. And in Kabul and Mazar-i-Sharif, men play music, women open their burqas and children fly kites. A taste for freedom starts to look like a universal value after all. The Pilgrim view [valuing personal freedom, responsibility, and self-determination] is prevailing not because it is Western or Christian, but because it is attuned to human nature."

Although no one can accurately foresee just how the world will reconfigure as the current situation plays itself out, it is certain that America will have a comprehensive involvement in the overall process. The imperative has been laid in our hand, and we really have no choice. The first step toward tomorrow is the annihilation of every party with a supporting role in the infernos of September 11. *After that,* we can sit down and discuss with the world the broader grievances that concern it. America does strive to exalt kindness (not consistently or adequately, but as a consensus-value nonetheless). But the world respects kindness only from those it fears.

Our generation is now defined by this crisis of transition. What kind of America will we hand to our children? Since the road will never lead back to where we once were, our only option is to face the mountain and climb.

Perhaps my effort will have no impact on the national discussion. I can live with that. What I could not live with was a failure to make any effort at all. Thomas Ridge has challenged: "We will find something for every American to do."

Mr. Ridge, I have done what I could.

Printed in the United States
1377800002B/64-255

9 781594 671944

America's Answer

This book presents a bold and workable formula for dismantling the mental resolve of Islamic warriors who have embraced the doctrine that asymmetrical warfare will bring America to its knees.

I regard the idea of a "decades-long war" against Islamic terrorism as obscene. Why should we hand to our children an unfinished job? The enemy has a fatal vulnerability that he cannot defend against. I have argued that we have no demonstrable justification for failing to seize our enemy in this softest of spots, and for holding him hostage with a formidable declaration of our capacity and intent with regard to his weakness. There is no difficulty in establishing the vulnerability of the horrifically murderous Islamic warriors. The difficulty is in liberating our own logic from the restraints of a humanist idealism that dulls our senses to the legitimate demands of action in a violent world.

This book is an offering of knowledge and ideas to America, with the aim of urging our national discussion in the direction of more aggressive and promising solutions to the threat confronting us. Our "patient accumulation of successes" offers no realistic hope of ever destroying the inner source of this threat to the security of our people and to the prosperity of our interests worldwide. My effort is in the direction of a more promising solution, and I believe the formula expounded in this book is viable, realistic, and necessary.

—*J. Patrick Griffin, Jr.*

J. PATRICK GRIFFIN, JR. is a self-taught student of world history and current affairs. He is the author of *Dispensationalism: A Biblical Examination* (published and available at PublishAmerica.com), a critical study of a dominant movement in mainstream Protestant theology.

ISBN 1-594671-94-X

90000

9 781594 671944